Also by Jonathan Sheppard

Someone Sinister
Bad Stories
Universe Unraveling
The Night I Died and Other Poems

This is a work of fiction. Names, characters, businesses, places, events, locales, and incidents are either the products of the author's imagination or used in a fictitious manner. Any resemblance to actual persons, living or dead, or actual events is purely coincidental.

BAD STORIES. Copyright © 2014, by Tyree Jonathan Sheppard. All Rights Reserved. Printed in the United States of America. No part of this book may be used or reproduced in any manner whatsoever without written permission except in the case of brief quotations embodied in critical articles and reviews. For information, email info@badthoughtspublishing.com.

ISBN-13: 9780692226636 (Bad Thoughts Publishing Company)
ISBN-10: 69222663X

Bad Stories

Jonathan Sheppard

Bad Thoughts Publishing Company
Los Angeles, Ca, USA

Bad Thoughts Publishing Company
Los Angeles, Ca, USA

www.badthoughtspublishing.com

Table of Contents

7   Letter From the Author

11   The Story of Googol

17   Slow Down! (This Is What Happened)

93   A Remote Mind

103   The Art of Chaos

137   Trust Your Lover's Phone

155   One Last Sunday

Letter From the Author

    I never thought that I would publish any of the proceeding short stories. In fact, it was only when I started to take myself seriously as a poet and writer that I thought that my work was worthy and it wasn't just the seething confidence of alcoholism. I just wrote. Something compelled me to tell these tales to myself on paper then share them with those similarly intrigued. I feel like a proud mother, I birthed life into the perils of chaos, free to be ridiculed or praised, embraced or disregarded with the choice to be oblivious to it all or be consumed by the endless bombardment of failure. "Why the fuck did I write this bullshit? I need to stop!" That's what I feel when I create anything, I can't choose how I feel I can only react but no matter what feelings are stirred I cannot stop creating.

    That thought is very self-indulgent because I am calling myself an artist. "Artist" seems like a title that should be bestowed upon you like you're being knighted, but still, I feel like a guitar player strumming or a painter stroking or a sculptor chiseling. It isn't the final product it's the fact that the artist takes an idea from its spiritual realm, an alternate reality, an ethereal of experience and emotion that many if not all people traverse but few revisit. The artist is the creator, the curator of simulacra that reminds others of their happiness way back when or their depression now. The artist is inspired by a myriad of muses to spend prized hours in attempts to make that inspiration tangible.

    The proceeding short stories undoubtedly pillage the truth. They are embellishments of events that probably have happened in my life. Every story, except for the *Story of Googol*, *A Remote Mind*, and *One Last Sunday* have some basis in events that I have experienced as I remembered them.

For,
Me.

The Story of Googol

Two incredibly brilliant men turned millions of years of evolution into billions of dollars in revenue. The tiny little backs of the preeminent urban pest are responsible for the answer to every question that you could ever possibly pose. From "How to" to "When was" and "How old is" to "What happened to" and even "Where is Osama bin Laden?" A secret CIA document posted on WikiLeaks expels how OBL was found through a Google Search and his location disclosed within three feet by Google Maps. The pests responsible for Osama's demise and the rapid acceleration and ease of access to information over the past 30 years are roaches, your favorite insect (or whatever the fuck it is!) to eradicate. The unwanted amenity to your urban living, the one worry you have when renting an apartment or spending the night over someone's place, the "I hope they don't have roaches or I hope I didn't bring any roaches with me" thought.

In a poorly maintained, shanty Palo Alto apartment building Larry Page, along with his roommate Sergey Brin, devised an information revolution, a search engine that made *Yahoo!* look like it was created by a bunch of cow tipping, hay shoveling, tornado dodging, farming... yahoos. Larry found himself under an unrelenting swarm of the only enemy indomitable to planet Earth's wrath. Mr. Page soon realized that if Mother Earth couldn't destroy the infinite epidemic then he was fighting a battle that he was sure to lose. Not even *Raid Max* could aid his efforts. Being the inquisitive and entrepreneurial fellow he was he thought, "How can I gather the most information encompassing every aspect of the human experience in the most efficient, far reaching, and intruding manner possible? While making use of these little irritating fuckers who keep getting into my cereal." Thought continued, "Without being detected and do it better than those shitty Yahoos!"

Larry's good friend and roommate was Sergey Brin. Sergey and Larry, were students at Stanford University. Sergey (or Dr. Brin) was a computer scientist. His Ph.D thesis was a 2,000 page essay on the use and benefits of Nano Technology. Dr. Brin created a microchip small enough to be placed on the wings of the most immature
and minuscule roach. Sergey never intended for these chips to be placed on the wings of roaches. He was originally commissioned by the NSA (National Security Agency) to develop a digital storage space small enough to fit in a camera the size of a hamster's balls and have a capacity large enough to hold hours upon gigabytes of video and audio information. That is exactly what Sergey did. Sergey refined an information retrieving system so advanced that the future couldn't even happen without his technology. That is to say that this story would have never been written.

  One microchip that only a very powerful microscope could register can be placed on the wing of a roach and also hold a half terabyte of digital information. If you're dealing with a cockroach that's about one or two inches in length then you can fit about 30 microchip video cameras/information processors per wing; initially. Sergey's microchips got smaller and more efficient. Each chip still maintained 500 gigabytes of digital space but instead of 30 video processors per wing it ballooned to an
almost incalculable amount. This is how the name *Google* was derived. LP and Dr. Brin discovered that a "google" amount of microprocessors could be placed on the wings of a cockroach. A "google" is the number one followed by 100 zeros (neither were English Majors and
they misspelled googol), so there was no limit to the amount of information one cucaracha could gather. Billions and trillions of roaches equipped with this technology could document everything that has ever come into existence and

make attainable through a search, the future. A cockroach in the sewer feasting on feces can determine the eating habits of a certain area while also processing the ingredients that it took to create the meal that created the excrement (the explanation for every recipe known to humanity being available through a Google Search). A cockroach is also responsible for most of the filming for *Bum Fights, Ghetto Fights, Girls Gone Wild, Bang Bus* and every other voyeur phenomenon.

The reason why humanity is aware of Chris Brown's birthday is because a roach was watching him cut his cake and counted the amount of candles he blew out. Society is aware of Cher's continued existence because she is Queen of all the roaches and can never die. A roach reminds elementary students everywhere that there is a North and South Dakota. Roaches are even responsible for every single album leak in the digital age. You got the latest Kanye West album three weeks in advance of release because a roach sat in on his private studio sessions. A runty camera on the wings of a roach eying your Big Mac captured your favorite fight inside of a McDonald's.

Everything from the fabric content of your favorite sweater to the release of a cell phone three years from now a roach is on top of it. Larry and Sergey placed the information that they gathered from the backs of those devilish bastards and placed it into a huge server database accessible by anyone who has the Internet. Google (googol) was born off the backs of the vilest, most despicable, and pestilent creature ever created. Before you destroy the next roach that crosses your path's gross, disgusting, odious and nuisance of an existence remember that it may carry the information that you need to impress at your next dinner party. Send your thank you cards to Larry Page and Sergey Brin for the cockroaches continued existence. They were endangered until 1997 the year of inception for Google's empire.

16

Slow Down!
(This Is What Happened)

One day in the arid, temptation ridden, desert of sensation that is Las Vegas, Nevada, a group of longtime friends, parched, prayed for the grand elation and release that is the neon landscape's infamy.

...

"I'm not trying to go to Tao tonight. I heard that the rage is at Marquee. It's at the new City Center, the Cosmopolitan Hotel. They just opened that shit recently. We have to be there, victories are already in hand," argued David.

"We're going to Tao bro. Tony, Jonny, Malik and I went there last time we were here. It's about to be insanity! Truly, it doesn't matter what club we go to tonight. We're about to have a good time no matter where the fuck we go. It doesn't fucking matter," Turner urged as he did not want the group to be split apart on their first night.

"I'm trying to go to Marquee too," interjected Mark. "There are about to be some prime females waiting and willing. Y'all can do what you want but Dave and I are going to Marquee."

"Why are you trying to split up the group? Let's just go to Tao," inquired Jonny.

"Yeah. It does not matter where we go tonight. It doesn't really fucking matter. We need to stay together," Tony agreed, reiterating Turner's point.

"Our cab is already downstairs. We're out."

"Where the fuck are y'all even going right now? It's only three o'clock in the afternoon."

Without giving an answer David and Mark left the sixth floor hotel room to their cab that was waiting in front of the main entrance of the Caesar's Palace Hotel and Casino.

"Them niggers had a plan and it didn't include us."

"What about you Will? Are you trying to go to Tao tonight?" Will is a six feet four inches tall mammoth of a man his three hundred pound frame dwarfed only by his size fifteen Converse Chuck Taylors.

"It doesn't matter as long as we hit the tables before... I'm trying to come up," Will admitted before he drank his second Five-Hour Energy shot.

"Whoa Will, you might as well have snorted an entire 8-Ball. Stop drinking that fucking poison."

"Yeah bro, why the fuck did you buy those? Vodka-Redbull, that's all you need. You're trying to go too fucking hard, too early. Calm that shit down."

"Fuck y'all! I've only had two."

"Yeah, in ten seconds you dumb ass."

"I'm good. Let's go though… We're about to fucking rage!"

What was left of the pack; Will, Turner, Malik, Jonny, and Tony headed downstairs to the Caesar Palace's casino.

They had all recently arrived in the sinful city all but Mark and David who had flew in the night before. Jonny had just arrived on the Greyhound from Los Angeles. Turner, who drove up from San Diego, picked him up from the bus station. Whilst Tony, Will, and Malik had landed two hours earlier at McCarron International also from Seattle, their hometown, Turner's and Jonny's as well. They then took a cab from the airport to the hotel room they had booked since last August.

The group, except for Will, had all known each other since high school, they had classes together, played in basketball games, ran in track meets and participated in leadership camps. They all gravitated naturally towards each other and remained great friends even after high school and even after Jonny and Turner moved to Southern California.

The lines of communication they had developed with one another had never been severed. High school was five years behind them now. Some of them just finished with their Bachelor's Degree others were a mere quarter or some years away, Mark was the only graduate student. He was pursuing a career in Dentistry.

At the University of Washington is where Turner then Malik and Mark had met Will who sat at blackjack table twenty-three jittery but intense, focused like an engraver of diamonds.

"Hit me… one more… stay," Will smoothly chopped towards his cards, his hands a warm knife through an ice cream cake.

"Three, Ace, Three, Jack, Queen. Dealer busts."

"This is easy. I'm about to pay for my whole trip right fucking now… stay."

"Six, Six, Jack… Dealer busts."

"This weak ass Dealer doesn't know what the fuck he's doing. This is too goddamn easy for me right now. Blackjack has some of the best odds in Vegas. Deductive reasoning is all you need. You have to know how many decks the Casino plays with. But it doesn't matter. Maybe, a Casino has a machine that continually shuffles decks, essentially an infinite number of decks; the odds are that the cards played still won't show again because they've been played. Find all the ten cards shown. Note the Aces. Then make a decision based on the likelihood of another big number card hitting. Say if I had seventeen to nineteen. I'm asking for another card almost every time…"

"Nigger, you aren't saying shit right now! You're guessing bro. You know you are. Get up so I can play," Malik and two Vodka Redbulls claimed, "Get the fuck up! It's my turn."

"Nah... I'm playing at least one more hand. Back the fuck up. There are a shitload of other tables, go play over there." Will then pointed towards a blackjack table with no patrons and a Dealer who seemed uninviting and rigid like he was anxious to end his shift.

"Fuck that shit! I want to play here with the shitty ass Dealer."

"Malik, he's coming up right now."

"Yeah he hasn't lost a hand yet," argued Tony and Turner in succession.

"Fuck it and fuck you guys. Let's put in on the next hand then. I got twenty dollars on it."

Jonny, Tony, and Turner all agreed to bet twenty dollars with Will who seemed to know what he was doing. He was up four hundred fifty dollars from one hundred early in his bout with the casino's of Las Vegas, who may not be undefeated but have an incredible Harlem Globe Trotter like win versus loss record. The alcohol flowed to the table like the Colorado into Hoover Dam, Malik and Will's kidney's the reservoir. Will had won many rounds with chance and his confidence in winning another hand festered. Nothing breeds confidence like winning and there is no one more infallible than a winner who is drunk. Will's jacket pockets were full of little bottles of Stolichyna vodka. There were four empty bottles on the table next to his chips that he had chased with a Monster Energy Drink and a Moscow Mule.

"Fuck twenty dollars! Give me everything that's in your goddamn wallets right... fucking... now!"

"You're not getting shit, else bro. My twenty is in your hands. Just win... this... fucking... hand," chuckled Tony who understood Will's demand as a joke.

"You aren't getting a single dime, fuck boy," Jonny dismissed his statement.

Turner, "Nah."

"Fuck y'all!"

Whilst Malik grabbed his share of the bet he contracted from his wallet, Will had grabbed the other two hundred dollars, which he quickly changed into chips with the dealer. Emphatically and with a realtor's confidence Will told the dealer, "All in," as he pushed all of the chips into the center of the crescent moon shaped table.

"You're fucking tripping right now. Give me back my fucking money... Fuck that shit my nigger. Give me back my shit!"

"Calm down fuck nigger. You're about to come up right now, pay for some of your fucking trip."

"Fuck you, you fucking clown! Give me back my fucking money. Sideshow Bob feet having bitch!"

Will calmly told Malik who he had just robbed, "If I lose, I'll pay you two to one."

Malik pondered, "If you lose you owe me four hundred forty bucks? If... you... lose... this... fucking hand your bitch ass fucking owes me four hundred forty American fucking dollars! Do you understand that you big grizzly sloth motherfucker?"

"Do you want to win Malik? Shut the fuck up bitch nigger. I got this."

The Dealer deals. Malik, Jonny, Tony, and Turner are huddled around Will watching every card as it is flipped with the anticipation of having to take a piss whilst driving but the next exit on the freeway is five miles away.

"Should we stay guys? Should we stay?"

"Hell yeah! We about to come up!"

They were dealt the Queen of Hearts and the Queen of Spades.

"We got this shit!"

"Let's go!"

The Dealer, "three" each card being turned over slowly, each agonizing turn of the cards told the group why the Caesar's Palace Casino made hundreds of millions of dollars last year, it told them that losing is inevitable, it is necessary, it will happen.

"Two."

"I told you motherfuckers..."

"Six."

"We got this you fucking assholes. Y'all don't know shit!"

"Seven"

"We got this shit! I got all the fucking drinks tonight. Bottle service and everything... strip club... we fucking those broads too..."

"Ahh, Let's fucking go!"

"We're about to come up!"

"Three. Dealer wins."

"Fuck..." Will exhaled as if he attempted to absolve the pain of a needle's small pinch.

"You have to be fucking kidding me! This motherfucker turned over a million cards and still got to twenty-one? Fuck gambling!" Jonny lamented.

"At least I only lost twenty bucks," Tony said as he looked over at a despondent Malik.

"You can't beat the casino. Only fools think that they can," Turner rationalized.

Malik sat behind the group invested in his own madness and then with the aggression of a hippopotamus approached Will who sat head in his hands on the center stool of blackjack table twenty three.

"Will you sorry piece of shit! Come up out your motherfucking pockets! That's four forty you fucking owe me. Put that shit in my hands, right... fucking... now, right now! You loser ass bitch! You owe me four hundred forty dollars! I said twenty motherfucker, twenty! You big ugly ass Sasquatch son of a bitch."

"I ain't paying you shit! You wanted to win. We all wanted to win. Fuck you, fuck nigger…"

Will then stood up, now face-to-face with Malik who was six feet one and two hundred ten pounds. Not a small man but next to Will's obesity seemed infantile.

"I'm not paying you shit fuck nigger! I ain't paying you a goddamn thing!"

"Ay, you owe me bitch ass nigger…" Before Malik could finish his scathing dissatisfaction Will had him in a choke hold.

Malik struggled and attempted to break Will's hold but couldn't as he gasped for breaths, "You… you stole my fucking money. You fuck… ing… owe me… you…bitch… ass… nigger!"

Jonny, Turner, and Tony sat in disbelief, entranced by how quickly the spat turned violent. They soon intervened and separated the two.

"I got you Malik. Fuck it! Money ain't shit! I'm going to pay you fuck nigger. I'm going to pay. You didn't really want to win though. You're not a fucking winner, fuck nigger. I'm about to pay for everyone's trip with this shitty ass fucking dealer right now," Will said as he sat back down at the blackjack table.

Malik walked over to Will and in his ear whispered loudly, "You owe me you fat fucking clown. You better fucking pay me. That's all I have to say."

The commotion didn't seem to grab the attention of anyone who worked the casino floor, security included, none of the gamblers put down their drinks or cigarettes to watch the event in a city where fights are its greatest spectacle.

"Here Malik. Here's one hundred fifty dollars. I'll give you the rest later."

"Alright, bro…"

"Damn it's still early. Fuck gambling… This shit is boring. We still have to find some females for the club tonight. Let's do that," Tony said in an attempt to quell the tension and awkwardness.

"Yeah I'm fucking with that. Let's go shopping too. I'm trying to be extra fresh tonight," said Turner.

"Nigger, I brought the interview clothes. You niggers are trying to spend cheese to kick it out here. No one gives a fuck about what you're wearing in these dark ass clubs, but I'm trying to get the fuck out of this casino too."

"Jonny, you're a fucking idiot and you don't know shit. Look at what you're wearing. Females about to run away from you," said Turner passingly, "They have some good shops and shit at the Venetian. Let's walk around over there. See what we can find. I'm trying to be fitted tonight."

"Corny ass niggers…" Jonny whispered under his breath as he shook his head in disgust.

"I need a shirt, I'm with it," Tony admitted.

"Yeah same here. You're tripping Jonny. You paid to come out here, this might as well be a special occasion get fresh you bum ass nigger. Have some fucking fun you sorrowful piece of shit," Malik said as he put one hundred and fifty dollars into his wallet and disregarded being in a chokehold.

"You niggers want me to watch you try on clothes? That's what you want. 'Oh this looks good doesn't?' That's some fuck nigger shit… but I'm with it. I'm tired of watching Will not know shit about blackjack… I'm thirsty maybe they have a liquor store somewhere."

"Fuck you niggers. I'm staying. I came here to win some motherfucking money," Will said holding a King and two Threes, "Hit me up when you fuck niggers are about to head back to the hotel and get dressed for tonight. I'll be right-fucking-here paying for ten of these trips."

"You better win me my fucking money. That's all I give a fuck about."

The best of friends left Will, exited Caesar's Palace and walked the few hundred feet to the Venetian. Jonny, Turner, Malik and Tony walked around Las Vegas' Italian simulacra in awe of the movie set feel as if a Hollywood production company had been commissioned. More importantly they relished in their camaraderie. This had been the first time that the four of them had been in the same city at the same time since they all visited Jonny in Los Angeles two years earlier. From shop to shop they joked and laughed and still knew each other like they met at a bar at least one night a week back in their native Seattle to talk about their wives and kids and jobs. Each, but a protesting Jonny, searched for outfits that would help to ensure that their first night in the city of inhibitions was as enlightened and worthy of the fairy tales spoken of it.

"Vegas is on some other shit! Look at all these people getting fucked up right in front of us," Jonny said as if that wasn't the biggest allure of Las Vegas, a prime vacation locale for a group of friends who loved to drink to get fucked up drunk beyond any scientific limitations.

"You've been here before Jonny. You know how it is."

"Look at this broad. She's drunk as fuck, stumbling, she almost fell into the canal. She's sloppy but she's getting it cracking right now," said Tony.

"Shit, I know where I've been, fuck nigger, I'm just saying… and that's the level I'm about to be on in about fifteen minutes. What the fuck have I been doing that I'm not drunk yet? Will was having fun because he was faded. I'm about to go in here and buy a bottle."

"I'm two drinks deep. Get on my level hoes," teased Malik.

"Will was about to beat your drunk ass though," replied Turner.

"Eat a dick, he's paying me my money so I don't give a fuck."

Jonny went into the liquor store wedged between an H&M and a Foot Locker.

"We'll be in here," Tony called to Jonny as he, Turner and Malik entered the Swedish, fast and disposable fashion chain.

"What do I want to drink? What the fuck do I want? Something good, something to celebrate being here with my niggers," Jonny said aloud to himself as he walked around the liquor store that seemed to contain every vodka, rum, tequila, whiskey, and scotch that has ever caused a fight or pickled a kidney.

"What do you like to drink?" interrupted the young associate behind the counter who seemed to have turned twenty-one years today, if it so happened that he was twenty-one.

"I like to drink a lot of Jim Beam maybe some Makers Mark, something dark, in the family of whiskey, bourbon, and scotches. I think I want something oaky... yeah something smooth and oaky. Preferably a scotch."

"Well, I don't know what your budget is but I really enjoy the Glenlivet Fifteen Year, oaky flavor with a little hint of spice. It isn't really a party drink though. It's meant to be savored, enjoyed."

"Every drink is a party drink, if you drink enough of it, but fuck it! I'll take that. I usually fuck with the Twelve Year which is a fucking great Single Malt for its price."

"Yes, it is exceptional, especially for its price. That will be seventy six dollars and sixty six cents, please sir."

"Sir? And goddamn, Y'all trying to break a nigger's pockets! I'm on vacation. I don't give a fuck," Jonny reasoned.

"That's usually the attitude around here."

"Here you go."

Jonny paid with two tens and three twenties.

"Thank you. Let me get you your change."

"You actually live here in Vegas?"

"Yeah, born and raised," the clerk said with pride and zeal.

"How the fuck do you live here? It's a cultural black hole. There is no way in hell I could spend more than three days in this piece of shit city. Outside of the Strip it looks abandoned, like a ship at the bottom of a dried ocean."

"It's all I know… Here's your change. Enjoy your time here and don't sink, sir."

Jonny smiled condescendingly then went into H&M to find the rest of his cohorts. He found Malik and Turner in the Men's section, both looking at jeans. As he walked up to the two he pointed at the manikin next to them dressed in a black blouse, white tie, a blue cardigan sweater, and plaid pants and said as he took a large gulp from the already opened bottle of Glenlivet, "You niggers trying to dress like this, huh? Just ask one of the shitty associates to get this for you and let's go find some broads."

"Bitch!" Turner called Jonny as he snatched the bottle from him and took a huge swig equal to Jonny's.

"Ay, dress like this tonight. I know this is the outfit you're about to buy. Look at this nigger in the church shoes," Jonny pointed at the manikin's feet, "Buy this fit. This is the outfit they want you to buy. Buy this bullshit. Buy this and let's get the fuck out of here."

Turner hands the bottle back to Jonny, "You're tripping right now. Calm the fuck down, go sit in the corner or something cry baby bitch. We'll be done in a minute."

"Fuck you bitch ass nigger! Where the fuck did Tony go?"

"I think he went to go look at some shirts or maybe he's at Foot Locker."

"I'm about to go look for him. Y'all have fun dressing like fucking manikins. Sheep ass niggers!"

"You ain't shit Jonny," Malik and Turner said in succession.

Jonny walked out of the store and towards the Foot Locker, passed a group of homeless kids in front of the chlorine blue channel that split the Venetian mall like a masochist's veins.

Jonny overheard, "He's drinking Glenlivet 15. He has good taste… but him having that bottle seems awful."

"That manikin is fitted though. Jonny doesn't know shit!" said Malik.

"Yeah, but I wouldn't wear it like that. Get those shoes the fuck out of here!"

"You find something yet? I'm about to go pay for this shit."

"Yeah, I'm ready too but I want to try some of this shit on first, see how it fits."

"Hurry the fuck up nigger. I'm trying to hit that bottle and the tournament starts in like thirty minutes too."

"Oh shit I almost forgot about that shit. I'm going to try this shit on and then we need to hit the Sports Book. I need to get this parlay in before the Louisville game."

"I'll be in line."

Turner and Malik understood that if how you look informs your mood then there is nothing more debilitating than being dressed like Jonny, also, in their experience women tend to be attracted to well-dressed men. After they both had paid Turner called Jonny so they could meet up and head to the Venetian's Sports Book. He didn't answer. As they exited H&M, Malik saw them next to an attendant who ushered tourists onto boats that attempted to make them feel as if they were traversing the Grand Canal in Venice, Italy.

Jonny was laid out on the ground in laughter's suffocating bosom. Tony was in a pair of snakeskin cowboy boots and a cowboy hat; he had tucked in his t-shirt. He looked as if he was impersonating the Marlboro Man for an in store promotion celebrating lung cancer. Both had commandeered the storefront of Wrangler's Express, they crowded the small entrance of the store, which specialized in boots, hats, and belt buckles specifically for the "California Cowboy."

Tony greeted people who walked passed with his best John Wayne impression, "Howdy there, partner… Now get the fuck out of here varmint. Mosey along now, go on and mosey."

Tony approached a group of young beautiful women all held yard long cups filled with margaritas. He told the brunette in the high wasted short pants and white tank top leading the way, "Give me your cup." The young brunette gleefully obliged, her friends laughed as Tony took a sip of the margarita from the straw.

"Now that's a rat writ, writ for a rat."

"You're crazy and cute cowboy, is that John Wayne?" Said the brunette who attempted to contain her giggle.

"Well now, what do you drink?" Tony ignored her question.

"That is John Wayne… I'll humor you only because you're so handsome… I'm partial to a lot of tequila, varmint."

"We don't have none of that, we don't have lemonade neither…" Tony then grabbed the bottle of Glenlivet, which was distended from his back pocket.

"I love Glenlivet," said the brunette's skinny blonde friend. She was pretty and pale, five feet eight inches tall and slender, she wore a black tank top with black leggings, which made her seem as an exclamation point in the Venetian's faux clouds.

Jonny was on his feet; he walked towards the group of young women and Tony, and as he wiped tears of laughter from his choked, bright red face, "That's one of my favorite single malts," he then acknowledged the other four women in the group with a coy smile.

"So you're a woman of scotches huh? What are some of your other favorites? Maybe we can go half on a bottle…"

Turner and Malik couldn't believe what they witnessed and stood aimlessly outside of H&M.

"Look at these niggers. They already found some women to help us get into Tao tonight, and from here they look good as fuck. Let's go over there. It's about to go-fucking-down!" Malik spoke with elation and security.

"Yeah we're about to get it cracking nonetheless… and if not them there are plenty of other fine ass women walking around this godforsaken city. We need to get to this fucking Sports Book though…" Turner focused on the NCAA Men's Basketball Tournament's opening weekend and the possible winnings.

"We have some time you're too anxious bitch ass nigger. Let's go see what these females are talking about."

By the time Turner and Malik made it to Tony's coral, formal greetings had already been shared and Kristen the brunette was putting her phone number into Tony's phone whilst Darcie, the blonde, whispered hers into Jonny's ear as he typed the number gaily into his phone.

"Well, we have to go now. It was so great meeting you Tony, Jonny," said Kristen as she gave Tony a hug.

"I told you we had friends," Tony said as he acknowledged Turner and Malik's presence.

"Yeah, and they're fucking cute too," said Karen who then turned around and giggled with Taylor and Kim.

"It was great meeting you beautiful ladies. I'm going to text you later."

"Please do, Tony. Maybe we'll all see each other later?"

"I hope we do. We better."

The young women walked away and as soon as they got out of the groups purview Tony jumped up and clicked his heels and threw the cowboy hat into the air. He shouted YEE-HAW loudly passed the painted clouds. Together, Jonny and Tony did the electric slide and 'dosey doed' in celebration of the beautiful women who they had met and the possibilities of what could come that night. The Wrangler's Express management looked on curmudgeonly as they waited for Tony to buy or return the store's merchandise; every mall patron within sight and earshot of the grandiose celebration joined them in awe.

"Let me go take this shit back to these clowns. YEE-HAW!"

"We still have to find more... many more females. Didn't the promoter say we have to have a 2-1 ratio to jump the line?" Jonny asked still glowing from the accomplishment of retrieving the beautiful blonde's phone number, "I hope she let's me fuck though..."

"You ain't fucking... and that's what the promoter said. We'll find them don't worry about that. Let's hit up the Sports Book. I need to get this parlay in right now."

Turner takes another drink from the bottle of Glenlivet then passes it to Malik; the bottle was now three-fourths empty. Malik tossed the bottle to Tony as he rejoined the crew and they continued towards the Sports Book.

...

David and Mark were at the Bellagio's Casino waiting for two women that they had met back home in Seattle. The two women, Alexa and Alyssa, were also in Las Vegas for the opening weekend of the NCAA Tournament, which is the biggest weekend for gambling receipts that, the city experienced all year. They had planned to meet up with the ladies they met at a Belltown nightclub as soon as their plane landed at McCarran International. David received a text message attached with a photo incentive from Alexa that forced them to the Bellagio, which explained David and Mark's urgency when they left the rest of the group.

"Ay bro, if these chicks don't hurry the fuck up… We have to make moves. I saw a couple of winners right when we stepped out of the cab. Should have cracked at them."

David rolled his eyes, "Calm down, Mark. This is a guaranteed victory. They're coming. They probably just want to look good for us. You know how long females take to get dressed and they just got here."

"Let's at least get a drink and go play some craps or something."

"I'm fucking with it."

As they walked through the Bellagio looking for the perfect craps table they see Will, he looked neurotic and agitated, he was drenched in sweat. His face adorned with the scowl of an unsatisfied glutton. He held a 5 Hour Energy Drink in his hand and they watched as he used it to chase a tiny bottle of vodka. He appeared quick and instinctive like a cat whose milk had been spiked with caffeine, determined to catch a long tailed rat trapped in a maze of cigarette butts.

"Will, what's up with you bro? Where are Turner, Tony, Malik and Jonny?"

"You look cracked out my nigger. What's going on?" A humored but undoubtedly concerned Mark asked.

"Yeah, Will you look like shit! You look like thick diarrhea chunks floating in shit brown water and bile," David echoed Mark's sentiment with comedic concern.

"Whatever bitch ass niggers. I gotta go. Let's get this money. I'm up thirty-six hundred right now, fuck niggers. Y'all ain't coming up, y'all ain't doing shit out here. Take those sunglasses off fuck niggers. Open your eyes to this money."

Will then jolted towards the poker tables in the back half of the Bellagio's Casino.

"That nigger is on some other shit right now. Somebody needs to save him. He needs to stop drinking that liquid heart attack," David told Mark as they approached craps table number thirty-three.

"You're dumb my nigger," Mark chuckled.

"Who has dice in hand? I want to play," David pulled out five one hundred dollar bills.

"Oh, this clown does? I think you just crapped out fuck boy. It's my motherfucking turn," David said to the patron who had just lost seventeen hundred dollars. He ascended to the head of the craps table like a king would his thrown. All of the other gamblers willfully appeased his desire to command the table and the dice.

"Y'all ready? Bet all your fucking money with me… Can I get three one hundred dollar chips and ten twenty-dollar chips? This for that fuck nigger Will."

David rolled the dice.

"Eleven. We have a winner."

"What the fuck did I say? Someone go get the waitress. It's game time!"

Mark inquired, "I heard you don't talk to them niggers Samuel and Dorian anymore. That's why Sam didn't come on this trip. Y'all used to be really close too. What the fuck happened?"

"Fuck them niggers man. I can't fuck with any snitch niggers. Why the fuck they telling my business? Were they trying to fuck my lady or something? What the fuck did they think; that she would become so vulnerable that she would fuck one of them or both? That's some fuck nigger shit! I had to mash Dorian for coming at me crazy one night."

Mark chuckled, "I remember you told me about that shit. That shit had me crying. I didn't know that it was about your ex though. I thought the nigger was just drunk as fuck and got too aggressive."

"Nah, nigger... well we were all pretty fucking drunk just chilling out at the apartment watching the Cotton Bowl, a nigger just made some wings and bought a shit load of beer had that VSOP on deck and shit..." David recalled as he shook the dice in his right hand then rolled them again.

"Point five!" The dealer relayed to the table.

"Let's go, five coming right-fucking-here... we were just drinking and watching the game, it was a good ass-fucking-game too. Auburn barely beat Nebraska. Then this nigger Dorian, drunk as fuck, comes at me crazy saying 'you fucked up man. You lost a good woman. What the fuck is your problem?' Getting all in my face and shit like he's going to fuck me up..." David rolled the dice again.

"Six!"

"Nigger had me fucked up. I was truly confused at first I didn't know where all this was coming from. This fool got serious after we were all having fun. But then I recalled coming home one day and Regina was on the couch crying. Talking some shit about me cheating on her with some broad I went to high school with. I told her I wasn't, because I fucking wasn't, but she saw some pics in my phone that some crazy ass broad sent me. You remember her, Tracey. Then she tells me that these niggers Sam and Dorian confirmed it. Our relationship was through after that…"

"Please, roll the dice sir… Nine."

"What happened between you and Dorian though, I know you destroyed him but what exactly happened… and where's that waitress at in this motherfucker? I should have had a goddamn drink in my hand already…"

David shakes the dice vigorously his arm stretched high above his head like "King" Felix Hernandez winding up for a pitch.

"Six."

"Goddamn it! Hit you bitch… well, this fuck boy was all in my face yelling at me trying to protect Regina like he was her boyfriend or dad or brother or some shit. I was like 'you better get the fuck out of my face Dorian. Watch the postgame coverage and chill the fuck out.' This nigger gets more rowdy and says, 'what the fuck man? I'm trying to help you out, why the fuck can't you listen to me. You fucked up!' Then that nigger grabbed my shirt like I was some little punk ass pussy kid with glasses he can just stuff in a locker…"

"Five, we have a winner."

"That took long e-fucking-nough, let's-fucking-go… But this nigger put his hands on me and as soon as he grabbed my shirt I fucking snapped. I grabbed his right arm and swung him around then threw that bitch ass nigger over the couch. Sam was there and so were Tony and Malik just staring not doing shit. I hopped over that couch like I was running from a dog and had to hop a fence my nigger. Then I gave that motherfucker the three-piece Chicken special. Nigger should have called me "Money May." Hit him two times with the right then hit him with an overhand left. The nigger stumbled back and fell through the coffee table. I picked that clown up and rushed him into the wall. The nigger was crying and shit. He ran into Sam's room like a hoe ass nigger. But fuck that my nigger, don't be putting your hands on me..."

"Seven, we have a winner."

"I'm heating up in this bitch! Y'all better bet with me tonight... then I started yelling at Sam asking him why he was telling my girl that I was cheating on her and other bull shit about me, trying to get me caught up. That bitch didn't have a good answer. He moved out the next week..." David then looked at gamblers who remained at craps table thirty-three and authoritatively said, "We're making some fucking money tonight."

He rolled again.

"Point three"

Mark sat at the table and cried tears of laughter as he placed his next bet with David's roll then finally the waitress arrived, she was a five feet seven inches tall Chinese woman. Mark knew she was Chinese because of the necklace she wore that said 'Love' in Chinese calligraphy, she was slender, a bit awkward but attractive enough to get Mark's attention. He liked that she was almost his height, only taller than her by a couple of inches.

"Three, you win again."

"David, what you trying to sip on?"

David looked at Mark like he should have already known. "Let me get a Hennessey and Coke please, two Henn and Cokes, thank you... how are you doing though, Marissa? You from Vegas?" Every worker in the casino had a nametag. The gentleman that worked the craps table thirty-three was also named Mark.

"Point six."

"No, I'm from the Bay Area, the Town to be exact. Anything else for you gentleman?"

"You're from Oakland? You know that Seattle is the Town now? Make sure you tell that to the people of Oakland next time you're there. But I would like you to take my phone number. I'm in town a couple more days and I would love for you to be the highlight of my vacation," Mark flirted.

"After one drink order? You're crazy," the waitress said as she blushed, her cheeks as red as the casino's carpet, "Get a few more drinks and you will certainly see me again..."

"Bring us each a Henn and Coke every 15 minutes. So you can get to know me."

"Six, we have a winner."

"Here's my card. I can't wait for my next drink... and it better be you that continues to serve us. Don't send one of your shitty coworkers unless she looks better than you. Don't send this nigger Mark either," Mark pointed at the dealer.

"I'm going to be here until at least midnight..." Marissa read the business card "Mark." She smiled bashfully then walked away indubitably uplifted from the advances.

"You see how we coming up? I'm trying to see if she has a home girl for you. We have to have a back up plan because these chicks are taking forever," Mark said accomplished.

"Where in the fucking hell are these females at? They need to hurry the fuck up! They're lucky I'm making some money right now. Otherwise, I'd be out of this bitch," David then contemplated the photo that was sent to his phone earlier, and then remembered what Alexa and Alyssa wore that fateful night in Belltown, "We can wait a little longer though, they're coming. We have drinks on the way."

Just then David received a text message.

"We're on our way down to the lobby. Sorry about the wait. ☺"

"Alexa just texted me my nigger. She said she's on her way down. And nigger, when did you get business cards?"

"I'm practicing for when I get my practice, I have to network. Hoes need their teeth fixed too."

They both laughed at Mark's crude proclamation.

"That's true… Finally our drinks," David still with dice in hand announced.

"Again, point six."

David and Mark sat around craps table thirty-three for three more rounds of Henn and Coke from Marissa awaiting Alexa and Alyssa's arrival.

...

At the Venetian's Sports Book Turner and Malik had placed their bets. Tony and Jonny were buying another bottle of liquor, the bottle of Glenlivet 15 year was empty and in the middle of the Venetian's mall canal where Jonny had thrown it.

"What did you buy this time Jonny? We need some light shit," Turner said with a thirsty look in his eyes.

"Go buy your own shit then fuck nigger! I stopped fucking with vodka a long time ago. No more vodka for me. I just got some more whiskey. Tony's bitch ass got some vodka though."

"Yeah, Tony already knows, vodka is for partying. Can't be drinking that dark shit. I become too destructive. Look at what you did Jonny. Why didn't you just throw the fucking bottle in the trash? That shit is for relaxing at home and getting some work done."

"Well, that's what I'm drinking all fucking night," said Jonny proudly as he held up a bottle of Johnnie Walker

Gold Label like he had just won MVP of the tournament. He took the bottle out of the box and then threw it at Turner.

"Real nigger drink!" Jonny opened the bottle and proceeded to bathe in the whiskey like he had just won a Bowl Game.

"I'm on that," Malik grabs the bottle from Jonny.

"I'm just saying, fuck the dark shit in Las Vegas. Once you taste this new drink concoction I make with the vodka, you'll change your bitch ass tune… let's go catch these games though…"

"Where y'all niggers trying to watch them?" Malik asked as he wiped whiskey from his lips.

"I don't know. But let's get the fuck out of this hotel, let's go to another place on the strip."

"Yeah, I'm good with that. Great-fucking-idea."

The tetrad exited the Venetian Hotel & Casino then paused as if to announce to the droves of lost souls who walked Las Vegas Boulevard that they had arrived. The souls responded obliviously. The sun was about to set and it became evident that the families there to see Barry Manilow or George Lopez or the Blue Man Group were taking their cameras, water bottles, and backpacks and abandoning the strip ahead of the night owls who would soon swarm the dusty strip, lost in purgatory unsure if they're up or down or just there. Ahead of those who only come to Vegas to drink, do drugs, and fuck, those who are scared of their inhibitions because of judgment back in their hometowns, cities miles away so they flock to Las Vegas and praise the insidiousness of secrecy and shun its revealer.

The wholesome families wade through a sea of flyers for escorts and strip clubs adorned with the bareness of everyone's favorite pornstar, trudge through the puke and piss and the feces of the many homeless and many more drunkards who use the city's laws as a reason to always have a drink in their hands, to avoid the raucousness that allows them to ponder why they chose Las Vegas, Nevada for their family vacation this year and every year since they've had children. Why they bring their families to a place that begs parents to answer questions from their children about their bodies and sexuality that they had hoped schools had already answered, the questions about drinking and alcoholism and destitution and obsession and greed and horrors that are baited; only to be framed and placed in photo albums, then denied and explained away as fantasy, as a fabricated copy of solvency.

The group eventually decided that they wanted to watch the NCAA Tournament at an establishment with chicken wings and a lot of televisions. Turner Yelped "wings" and Yelp suggested the Hooter's Hotel that was just off of the strip across from the back entrance of the MGM Grand.

"Damn! Weak ass Illinois! I knew I shouldn't have put that weak ass team on my parlay. Damn them to fucking-Hell... I gotta go make another parlay," said Turner in a rage.

"I told you. They aren't shit! Didn't touch that game on mine. I'm still alive I just need Xavier to beat weak ass Portland State and I'm up a grand."

"You aren't shit Malik."

"You don't know shit about basketball though, Turner. Go make another parlay you losing ass bitch!"

"I can't wait to eat these wings; you text that chick yet, Jonny? What about you Tony? Hit them up. What the fuck y'all been doing?"

"Nah, not yet. Did you text yours, Malik? Oh I forgot you don't have shit though!"

"I don't think I am..." said Tony, "Fuck them."

"Yeah I feel that, you barely know them. But we need some broads to help get us into the club tonight and we need guaranteed numbers. These clubs tax the fuck out of you and the lines are too damn long. We need assurance. I feel like I'm paying my rent when I pay to get into one of these shitty ass fucking clubs, I am not trying to do that."

"Fuck Illinois, goddamn it! Almost had five grand in my goddamn hands," Turner lamented, still, over the one game that ruined his parlay.

"Let me get some of that Johnnie Walker Jonny."

"I thought you were only going to start fucking with 'light' shit?" Jonny teased as he handed Turner the bottle.

"Don't drink that shit in here, Turner. We're in a business that sells alcohol."

"Fuck that. We all ordered beers already, didn't we? They got their alcohol money from us."

"Let's go Xavier! About to have some cash to blow tonight and call those fucking females.," Malik demanded of Tony and Jonny, "They want to hang out with y'all and I'm trying to get on with at least one of them."

"Food is here!" the very voluptuous waitress said interrupting their banter.

"Let me know if you handsome fellas need anything else, okay?"

"We will, thank you beautiful… I'm about to go to work on this fucking food. Don't say shit to me for fifteen minutes."

"Have any of you heard from Mark or David? I wonder what David and Mark have been up to?"

"They haven't been up to shit… Let's go Musketeers!"

...

David was up nineteen hundred dollars courtesy of crap table number thirty-three and Mark had won twelve hundred and a date Saturday night with Marissa the casino waitress.

Finally, they were in the company of Alexa and Alyssa. Both of the young women looked incredibly intoxicating and intimately provocative, enticing and bodacious. Mark and David seemed to forget that they had been waiting for them for more than two hours and the money that time bought.

Now they were in David and Mark's sixth floor Caesar's Palace hotel room, three doors down from the rest of their cohorts. Half a bottle of Hennessey and an empty pint of Hennessey VSOP rested on the queen sized bed closest to the hotel room's lone window with two half eaten large pizzas.

"Can we play some music?" And without waiting for an answer Alyssa walked over to the iDock in between the two queen sized beds that dominated the space in the room and plugged in her iPhone, which was already on the Gucci Mane Pandora station. She then grabbed the half empty bottle of Hennessey from the bed and took a drink; she closed the bottle and threw it to her girlfriend, Alexa. Before she could take a drink Mark grabbed the bottle from her hands and said, "It's my turn sexy… this is that shit right here. Turn this motherfucker up," Mark began to rap along,

"Rockstar lifestyle might not make it. Livin' life high everyday click wasted."

Alexa now had the bottle; she took a drink whilst grinding on Mark's lap the words shared on each other's lips like they had written the song together. In unison they rapped,

"Woke up in the morning ten o'clock drankin'… I'm so wasted, she so wasted. Tell the bartender send me twenty more cases…"

"This is the official Vegas anthem right here. Played this song like ten-fucking-times in a row on the plane here," David admitted as Alyssa danced on his lap on the edge of the queen sized bed near the room's exit like they were in one of the many gentlemen's clubs that populated Las Vegas. She faced him, David's hands caressed her shape, akin to the goddess Venus except her limbs and head were accounted for. David began gripping Alyssa's waist and became very aroused by her ample bottom gyrating and agitating his crotch and his cock.

Alexa's inciting dance with Mark had turned into kisses on his neck. She had unbuttoned Mark's shirt and exposed his bare chest, she undressed him incessantly and only stopped to share another drink with her lustful target.

"Alexa pass me that bottle, bitch. Trying to drink it all…" Alyssa demanded severing the trance that had possessed them.

"Shit, don't we have another bottle, David? Look in the freezer."

"Yeah it's in the freezer. Nigger, we're going to have to go to the liquor store soon. The four bottles we brought are almost gone. This is the last one," David said as he pulled a 750ml bottle of Hennessey VSOP from the freezer.

Alyssa interrupted, "I know you niggers smoke. I snuck some of that Grade A, top of the line, Seattle top shelf greenery onto the plane. We just need a Swisher or a blunt wrap or something… I really need to smoke before things get a lot more fun in here," Alyssa then pulled out an eighth, three and a half grams of marijuana, from her purse and passed the bag to David who then tossed it to Mark each smelled the worth of the product that Alyssa smuggled. It smelled infinitely valuable.

"Shit was already fun as fuck to me but I'm not opposed to some more fucking fun. I'll go downstairs and pick up a Sweet from one of the shops," David volunteered. Before he exited the hotel room he poured some Hennessey into a red cup.

"I'll be right back. Save something for me."

David then hurried to the elevator, which arrived to the lobby agonizingly slow.

...

Jonny, Malik, Tony, and Turner had just exited their cab from Hooters and were walking up to the main entrance of Caesar's Palace.

"What the fuck is that goddamn smell? Did someone step in shit? I stepped in some goddamn shit! You have to be fucking kidding me. Fuck this goddamn, fucked up, shit littered city," a visibly drunk Jonny yelled into the stale desert air. He then engulfed what was left of the bottle of Johnnie Walker Gold and hurled the bottle into the middle of Las Vegas Boulevard.

"Fuck this piece of shit city!"

"Uh oh..." Tony said as if it was the agreed upon warning sign that one of the quadruplets had become too intoxicated. It was a passing protest that was barely acknowledged but seemed undoubtedly cryptic.

"Quit crying and go wipe your feet in that grass over there. Don't track that shit into our room, fuck nigger."

"Fuck you! I'll use your tongue hoe ass nigger."

"You ain't shit though... what are y'all about to do? I'm going to the Sports Book to collect my winnings."

"Hold up Malik, I'm trying to make another Parlay. Jonny and Tony what about y'all?"

"I'm going up to the room to chill and get into this bottle of vodka. What time do we have to be at Tao to guarantee that we can get in? And we still have to find more females to come with us. The lines are insanity even at ten o'clock."

"The promoter didn't specify a time so I'm thinking as long as we're there by one in the morning we should be good. We can just grab some women from the line, I'm telling you. We're in there for sure. Hit up those chicks from earlier just in case and save me some vodka you motherfucking bitch ass bitch," Turner responded.

"I'll go up to the room with you Tony. I brought a bottle of Crown Royal with me on the Greyhound. I'm trying to get into that and watch tonight's last tournament game. I'm going to hit up Darcie's fine ass too. I'm fucking her tonight."

"You ain't fucking shit though… see y'all up in the room."

...

The group had split in half. On their way up to their sixth floor hotel room, Tony and Jonny saw David coming out of Caesar Palace's lone convenience store with a Swisher Sweet in his ear and a red cup in his right hand. The red cup was half full illuminated by the casino's lights like a Jack-o-Lantern.

"Look at this nigger right here. What the fuck you been up to and where the fuck is Mark?" Jonny asked David, his twin brother who was five inches shorter and sixty pounds lighter, as if he was in the midst of an intense interrogation.

"Man, just making money. I came up nineteen hundred at craps table thirty-three in the Bellagio; that'll be the table I'm click clacking at tomorrow. Number thirty-three all day! But Mark is up in the room right now with these two broads we met back home. They brought some fire down so

I'm picking up a few Sweets and we're about to make shit happen."

"Damn, you niggers are winning! You clowns had victories set-up before you even stepped on the plane."

"Yep, trying to knock these out the park so we can get some new women, some Vegas chicks, tonight. I have to go handle business though. When we finish with this we'll head to y'alls room for the turn up before the night begins."

"Have fun bro! And wrap it up, my nigger! Everything stays in Vegas except for STDs."

"Don't play me like that brother. You already know. See you niggers soon. Bet you niggers don't get any pussy this entire trip though."

"That's not my goal," Tony and Jonny said in unison.

David headed back up to the hotel room were Mark, Alexa, and Alyssa were drunk dancing and singing. When David approached the room door he could hear the trio singing at the top of their lungs,

"I'm on my grind shorty. Don't block my shine shorty. Hold up! Hold up! Guess who done showed up. Rolled up, post up, drop wit' the door's up."

David opened the door to Alexa and Alyssa, who were fervent and eager to smoke marijuana before David left but now were dancing on the bed closest to the window. They seemed subservient to the upbeat bass that littered the Big Boi and Gucci Mane song, their eyes closed, the words titillating to the freedom of their vacation. David's presence was generally unacknowledged by the jubilation of the young women. Mark saw David and swiftly approached him, seemingly transporting himself to within inches of David's face, he whispered in David's ear,

"My nigger. I'm about to put in some work. I need a condom though," attempting to hide his glee.

"Yeah I got one for you. They're in my travel bag in the bathroom. Damn, we're getting it cracking right now. Them other niggers missing out. I just saw them in the lobby."

"They know we all have to fend for ourselves out here. We caught ours. They have to catch theirs. I'm going to hit this bathroom real quick."

As Mark closed the bathroom door, David jumped on the queen-sized bed where Alyssa and Alexa danced. He pulled Alyssa close and pulled the Swisher Sweet from his ear, guiding it in front of Alyssa's face like she was a child and he was her father; playing "Airplane" with her food.

"Ooh, let's roll that fire up right now. This is some kill. I hope y'all are ready," Alyssa said as she snapped out of her trance, "A couple hits of this and we may not be going anywhere tonight." Alexa was similarly enthralled; she immediately recognized David's presence as her withdrawal's cure. They both hopped off the bed and sat at the room's only table.

When Mark left the bathroom Alyssa and Alexa were at the table rolling up a blunt and David was sitting on the bed, he sipped his second cup of their last VSOP bottle slowly and patiently. Anticipatory but subdued was David as he watched the University of Washington versus Mississippi State game. The music had been lowered and soothed the extraordinarily focused scene.

"This is a blowout. U-Dub is destroying these racist farmers," said David to Mark who had graduated from the University of Washington like Turner; Malik and Tony were not far from their Bachelor's Degree.

"I already knew they would. Game wasn't even worth watching that's why I didn't watch it. Who do they play in the next round? They'll probably play Purdue who they should beat but fuck Romar, shitty ass coach. U-Dub should have fired his ass years ago. So much talent he couldn't keep in state. Give him the fucking boot!"

David quickly renounced Mark's pick of his alma mater, "They won't win shit."

"What's going on? They rolling up the weed? I'm still trying to go out tonight. Do you know what they're trying to do?"

"I'm not sure. We haven't talked about that. Back home Alexa told me that they had a lot of plans this weekend. I think they're going to Bank or somewhere tonight. Alyssa told me that they have some homegirls flying into town tonight."

"Cool, that's perfect!" Mark whispered into David's ear, "They don't need to be anywhere near us after this. We have more hunting to do."

David laughed.

"She needs to hurry up and roll that shit. The waitress from the Bellagio hit me up while I was in the bathroom. She's trying to meet us at Marquee with three of her friends tonight."

"Maybe them and their homegirls are trying to come too though. They said they might go to Bank. We need a two-to-one ratio in every club we go to."

"I'm not worried about that. We aren't wedded to none of these females. The more the merrier. We're in there no matter what... What's good with that blunt though, Alyssa?"

"They're all ready. Can you pour me another cup of Hennessey please, Mark? Where's the lighter, Alexa? We can smoke these back to back to back if y'all want."

"Pour me one too, please Mark? And I have the lighter here. We shouldn't smoke our entire supply of weed on the first night. Save some of that. Tarren and Nicole should be landing right now and I don't think Tarren's bitch ass brought any with her. She was being a scared little cunt."

"Before you light that let me put a towel in front of the door."

The music still played softly as did the last NCAA Tournament game of the night. They then recoupled, each couplet with marijuana filled cigars and red cups filled with cognac by their side. They situated themselves evenly between the two queen-sized beds, and cuddled with the comfort of optimistic and elated couples on their honeymoon.

"What do you have planned for the rest of the night?" Mark asked Alexa as she lay on his chest and inhaled deeply the blunt smoke, she exhaled then answered, "We're just waiting for our friends to fly in. But I'm not even worried about that right now," Alexa then placed the nearly defeated blunt to Mark's lips, Mark inhales; she then throws the roach into an empty bottle on the nightstand. They share kisses as Mark exhales into Alexa's mouth. They kissed with the pain of distant lovers finally close enough to touch lips, Alexa exhales once more, and then they commence the sensual foreplay necessary for the best coitus.

David and Alyssa were already underneath the blankets of their bed engaged in the ruinous activity that consumes most of Las Vegas' tourists, that consumes most people.

...

When Tony and Jonny returned to the hotel room Will was dressed and ready to hit the town, he was drinking a Vodka & Redbull. His clothes were soaked; they looked as if he got dressed immediately after showering, and he was animate about using his outfit as a towel to dry his body.

"Y'all niggers aren't ready yet? I just won twelve thousand dollars playing poker. Y'all can't tell me shit. Where's Malik at? I'll choke that nigger out. I got his motherfucking money. Let's do it big... We're getting it fucking cracking tonight... Y'all better have hoes like I have this money, bitch ass niggers. I'll meet you niggers there all the bitches are waiting for me."

Will threw five hundred dollars at Tony and Jonny then stormed out of the room.

"That nigger is cracked out right now. At least he got Malik his money."

"I should keep sixty of it though. Malik wouldn't trip."

"Give him all of it."

"I was just kidding bitch... But one of us needs to grab him and let him know he needs to chill out, he needs to slow-the-fuck-down. But he won twelve grand. He's right, 'we can't tell him shit!' if that was me that just won twelve grand I'd be in the Philippines right now." Tony chuckled.

"Fuck the fucking Philippines, I'd be in Mexico or Colombia or somewhere coked out with too many fine ass women around me. The first night I'd cum so many times my balls would dry up. Wouldn't be able to have children for the rest of my life."

"You're a dumb ass, Jonny."

"Seriously though he's probably had enough energy drinks to turn a sloth into a motherfucking starving grizzly bear trying to protect her cubs from an asshole drenched in honey. He isn't trying to listen to us. Let's just get ready. He'll meet us there," Jonny said insensitive and dismissive of Tony's waning and insincere concern.

"I'm about to hop in the shower."

"Hurry the fuck up though, I'm next."

While Tony showered, Jonny took the bottle of Crown Royal from his duffle bag and grabbed one of the red cups that Turner brought, as soon as Jonny began pouring there was a knock on the door. It was Terrance who was the last of their high school companions to arrive.

"You niggers forgot about me. I thought Tony was supposed to use Turner's car to come get me from the airport?" Terrance angrily complained.

"That nigger is in the shower. You should have come into town earlier. And we're all drunk as fuck anyway. Have you ever been to Jail in Vegas? Thought so! No one is trying to ruin the night with a fucking DUI. How could any of us have fun knowing that Tony is in jail because his drunk ass went to go pick you up from the airport and we let him? But you're here now and you haven't really missed shit. We'll all be ready to hit Tao soon. Turner and Malik are downstairs at the Sports Book."

"Fuck you guys, I told y'all I had to work and couldn't fly in until late… Shit, I wore what I'm wearing tonight on the plane. I'm ready. I need a few drinks to catch up with you guys though. I know y'all have some drinks ready for me."

"You already-fucking-know," Jonny handed Terrance the cup of Crown Royal he had poured for himself then poured another.

Shortly after the Washington Huskies had beaten Mississippi State, Turner and Malik arrived at the hotel room and joined Jonny, Tony, and Terrance who were all dressed and ready to walk over to Tao. It was now forty-five minutes passed ten and Jonny was getting anxious to leave for the club as he had texted Darcie and told her that he'd meet her at Tao's entrance by eleven.

"Y'all need to hurry the fuck up and get dressed. We're about to leave."

"We'll be dressed in like ten minutes calm-the-fuck-down Jonny, bitch... Tony you still have that vodka? I'm about to make you motherfuckers my special 'Turn Up' cocktail..."

"This nigger... get dressed motherfucker. Let's fucking go! We don't have time for this bullshit!"

Turner grabbed a red cup and began to pour disregarding Jonny's protest, proudly he announced each ingredient to his raucous mixture, "Two shots of vodka, Red Bull, splash of cranberry juice, and a splash of orange juice. Let's go! Turn up!" Turner downed the drink like a shot and began to pour another, "Who else wants one? I'm about to put on some motherfucking music in this bitch. Let's get it cracking! We in Vegas doing it big out here! Nobody better tell me shit!"

"Ay, we have to make moves. We have to get these females because if we have to wait in line we might as well stay here," said Terrance who had recently arrived and looked as if he already had three too many drinks.

"Darcie and her home girls are waiting for us. I'm about to go meet up with them. I'll see you bitch ass niggers there."

"Jonny you're a trick ass bitch. We're good. Clubs stay open until like, 5:30AM. We're getting in. Jonny, Tony, they're meeting us there right? They aren't going anywhere. I bet we see them inside. A group of fine ass women that big should be able to cut the line with ease. We'll grab the females we need from the line. I know there are a lot of smaller groups of women that won't be trying to wait to get in. Grab any female, even the ugly ass fat fudge eating females."

"Darcie, man. You saw her... hating ass nigger. Don't fuck this up for me. And how are you so sure that these chicks will just walk in with us? You don't know shit," responded Jonny.

"Just tell them they can cut the line. Why wouldn't they want to do that? If a chick doesn't want to do that she needs to take her ass home. I'll buy her fucking plane ticket back to her shitty ass city. That doesn't make any sense to me. They may not want to go in with your bitch ass though, Jonny. Quit crying and Turn-the-fuck-up!"

"We'll be ready before then though. Calm down y'all," Malik promised, "Darcie's friends were fine as fuck Turner. You already know, and I want on."

"Fuck them! It doesn't matter to me. We get there when we do. Turner? What was that mix again?"

"See Tony isn't being a bitch like the rest of y'all, too many women in Vegas to be tripping this badly but I'll make you one. These clowns are tripping right now. Actually, I'll make one for everyone to calm us down. We're in Vegas motherfuckers!"

Two hours later Tony, Malik, Jonny, Turner, and Terrance ascended the Venetian steps to the front entrance of Tao Night Club & Bistro. Kristen nor Darcie would respond to either Tony or Jonny's text but the group composed themselves, hid there drunkenness the best they could, and approached groups of women waiting in line to get into the crowded disco. Turner and Jonny grabbed a group of three each, Malik a group of four and Tony a group of five. Terrance was sitting on the bench to the right of the line with his head in his hands fatigued from drinking what Jonny had drank all day in two hours.

"Terrance wake the fuck up and let's go. We in here."

"Make sure you don't fall asleep inside, pal!" the security guard warned Terrance.

Like a group of lionesses approaching a herd of gazelles the gang entered the nightclub, peering past the droves of young and stunning women they had corralled like tall African Savannah vegetation. The young men from Seattle and the women that helped guide them onto the plains parted ways and they were left uncovered, to fend for themselves.

"Why didn't we just try to hang out with some of them? A few of them were fucking incredible! We may not find some dimes like that all night. Really, you niggers aren't doing much better than them tonight," Terrance said as he yawned.

"Man, we just got here. If we see them again we see them again but I want to walk around first and weigh my fucking options. Let's go to the bar," said Malik as he led the group through the VIP section and to the back bar. The section was empty because 12:30AM was too early for Important People to spend thousands of dollars.

"Can I get five 'Turn Ups' and five shots of Patron?" Turner asked of the confused bartender.

"I'm sorry, what was that you said? A 'Turn Up?' I've never heard of that."

"It's Vodka, Red Bull, with a splash of cranberry juice and a splash of orange juice," Turner looked as if he had bestowed the most pondered and confusing universal truth upon the bartender.

"Coming right up!"

"You didn't have to get me a drink Turner but I'll take it," an accomplished Jonny told Turner as he showed him one of the flasks he carried.

"Shit, you can get the next round. You know I'm not tripping."

"I have three flasks on me right now. I'm not paying for a single drink in this motherfucker tonight. Y'all need to realize this. I've never been patted down in Las Vegas. I could have a fucking machete in my pocket. No one would ever know."

"What forreal? You're a genius for that. They don't ever pat you down or use metal detectors, do they? I would have never thought to do that. You should have filled them up with the 'Turn Up' though."

"I have Jim Beam in one. Crown Royal in the other two. I know you're a bitch ass nigger so you don't like dark shit but take one since you just spent three hundred dollars on drinks like a damn clown."

"I'll take it!" Turner then put the flask in the breast pocket of his blazer.

The bartender interjects, "That will be one hundred five dollars."

"Damn… Shit… You were close e-fucking-nough, Jonny! But we're on vacation right now and I don't give a damn… Close it out, please… Let's take these fucking shots and get our trip truly started! Y'all ready? Time to go hard! 'Turn Up' time!"

The group tapped shot glasses and cheered to a 'Great night' and as fast as the shots went down so did the 'Turn Up.'

"I have to go to the bathroom. Where you guys going to be?" Jonny asked, "This club is fucking huge, no way I'm finding you motherfuckers in here."

"Just text one of us," Tony told Jonny. That was the last time any of them saw Jonny for the rest of the night.

"You guys trying to go upstairs? Last time we were here I didn't explore every floor so I haven't really been in here but I know they have a pool and that it's on the roof."

"Yeah, let's head to the roof they have a different DJ on every floor too. That's probably where all of the women are anyway, near the fucking pool. "

"I see a lot of women all over. Take your pick. I'm trying to walk around down here for a bit I'll meet you niggers upstairs," Tony then split the crowd behind them at the bar and disappeared onto the dance floor. Malik, Terrance, and Turner then headed up the three flights of stairs to get to Tao's rooftop pool.

"Let's go to this bar back here, get another drink in us and then let's get to work. Whoever gets a chick back to the hotel room first wins... I got this round," Terrance suggested as he yawned one more time.

...

Jonny was still downstairs and he had just finished one of his two flasks in the men's bathroom. After he washed his hands he texted Tony. He didn't want to maneuver through the monstrous disco by himself. Tony would not respond so Jonny began to search for his friends. First he circled the first floor, cutting through the dance floor and once again through the VIP section, which was slowly began to fill. His phone's reception was terrible inside of the club so Jonny decided that he would make one more attempt on the first floor of the club before he stepped into the Venetian's lobby to see if he could get better phone reception to call one of his four friends. With flask in hand Jonny walked in a cautious stupor but to no avail. Tao was crowded like Figueroa Street in Downtown Los Angeles after the Lakers had won the NBA Championship or Capitol Hill in Seattle after Barack Obama had won the presidency. Jonny couldn't help but run into walls and patrons or bump into chairs and tables.

On his way out of Tao, Jonny was tapped on his shoulder and was spun like the top to a liquor bottle half opened. It was Darcie. She wore a bewitching black dress with midnight blue heels that matched her lipstick, toenails, and fingernails. Light from one of the clubs many disco balls reflected off of her plush lips like the moon on a calm ocean. Her sandy blonde hair shimmered in the dull and stale air of the club that should have been a fulfillment warehouse.

Jonny was speechless but a beautiful, despite her undisguised drunkenness, Darcie spoke for the both of them, "I thought you said eleven-o-fuckin-clock you goddamn asshole?"

She then grabbed the sides of Jonny's face and kissed him passionately and ferociously. She pounced on her prey that was too paralyzed to descent. Jonny snapped out of his daze and then began to return Darcie's vigor as she pushed him towards a VIP booth that seemed to be abandoned by its renters. They fell onto jackets and purses and knocked over the bottle of Belvedere Vodka that was half empty as well as the glasses that weren't finished being used. Darcie's right hand had left Jonny's left cheek and was in his pants arousing his manhood. Jonny had his right hand on her voluptuous ass which he grabbed like he was kneading dough and then his left fingers rubbed her sensuality unhindered by panties. His left hand pleasured her womanhood whilst his right crept to Darcie's neck in an attempt to control her chaotic kisses. As soon as Darcie began to unbuckle his belt, Jonny's lust subsided temporarily as it became evident that they were about to fuck in a large nightclub at the height of its capacity, although not a soul was privy to their unrestricted rendezvous. Even the group of young women who stood on the booth seats of the VIP table adjacent to their sexual ardor had no clue, all in the club consumed by the selfishness of their own pleasure.

"Darcie... Hold on... Darcie... I have a room all to myself right next door... I want to really enjoy you and feel you and taste you... I want your body to be mine only... my eyes, my hands..." Jonny then bit her left nipple through her dress.

"I want to fuck you right now, right here... right fucking now! Let's just do it. I was hoping I would see you again and I did. I'm not going to squander this opportunity. I want your fucking dick; I want to feel all of this... I need you to feel me tight around you..."

Darcie bit Jonny's bottom lip then kissed his neck as she had now unbuckled Jonny's belt and unbuttoned his pants but before she could pull down his zipper Jonny grabbed her hands.

"Let's go Darcie... my room is right next door. We can do anything and everything you please. Just be patient sexy and I promise that I'll give you all of me... you can have whatever you want... whatever you need..."

"Our room is right up stairs. Let's go... right fucking now. I'm either going to fuck your brains out right here or in my room. I'm not going anywhere else."

"I'll go wherever you want me to go, just lead me."

Darcie then dismounted Jonny and pulled him up out of the booth by the crotch of his pants that were now buttoned and held up securely. Jonny then smacked Darcie on the ass and grabbed her by the hair. He kissed her like he was on his way to war and his lips would never again be blessed by her beauty. She took hold of his hand and escorted him towards their predestined ecstasy.

As the two exited hand in hand Jonny pulled out his flask and offered it to Darcie who took a nice sized swig. Jonny partook then put the flask back in his pocket.

They walked passed the restroom twenty feet from Tao's exit, "Jonny, I'm so fucking sorry but I really have to use the bathroom. You made me way too fucking horny. Wait for me here, papa."

"Of course. We both have some fucking tension to relieve. I'm not going anywhere pretty lady."

Darcie cut the long line and went into the ladies restroom as Jonny waited on the wall between a bamboo plant and a picture that read, "Love is a prison" in Chinese calligraphy. Darcie entered the women's restroom door; just then he was bumped in the shoulder by a Tao security guard who was leaving the men's restroom. He was about five feet six inches tall he had very broad shoulders and had to weigh at least three hundred fifty pounds. His hair was in a ponytail he seemed as if he was some type of islander from Fiji, Samoa, or Tonga. Jonny at six feet three inches and two hundred twenty pounds towered over the stocky hired muscle. In a voice filled with absolute impunity and power the security guard said, "watch where the fuck you're going, ass wipe."

"Fuck you, you wild pig eating motherfucker! Watch where the fuck you're..."

Before Jonny could finish his insult he was pushed by the girthed security guard which caused Jonny to do a backwards barrel roll towards the Emergency Exit which was about fifteen feet from the entrance to the restrooms.

Jonny immediately sprung to his feet but as soon as they were set and he began to charge towards the security guard he had been rushed out of the Emergency Exit doors by the Islander and another much larger member of the Tao security personal. The Pacific Islander grabbed the right arm and a six feet six inches tall four hundred pound man whose size was his only distinguishable characteristic on his left. They threw Jonny through the emergency doors that led into a brightly lit hallway where Venetian security guards were waiting to escort Jonny off of the property.

"Come with us sir. You have to leave the premises immediately or you will be issued a trespass citation."

They were wore purple blazers and white blouses, with khaki pants their uniforms and Jonny's inebriation disguised any other distinguishable information to decipher. He saw only their jackets, the color of plums.

"Fuck that linebacker. That motherfucker started it. Y'all can check the tapes, I didn't do shit. You motherfuckers better not touch me. Fuck you, Purple Coats!"

Jonny then proceeded to kick and bang on the emergency exit door, demanding that he be let back into the club. The four Venetian security guards then surrounded Jonny in attempt to restrain him and contain his rage.

"You motherfuckers better take your motherfucking hands off of me right fucking now!"

The three Venetian security guards dropped their hands.

"Calm down sir. Please just exit the premises without making a scene."

"Making a scene? Bitch, I shouldn't have gotten thrown out in the first place, fucking bitch ass nigger, your security is shitty! Fuck it! I'm out of this shitty ass place. I'll spend my fucking money elsewhere."

He had completely forgotten about Darcie. Jonny was escorted through another set of double doors that opened to a long path that led to Las Vegas Boulevard.

"This place is fucking trash! Just like you Purple Coats. What the fuck are you guys supposed to be? I don't get it. You motherfuckers are trash too. Straight-fucking-garbage. Looking like Grimace. Where's Hamburgler and Ronald and all the other fuck niggers? I don't have any cheeseburgers you fucking clowns!"

A trashcan nearby became the focus of Jonny's rage as he began kicking the receptacle in order to knock it over but it was bolted to the ground. Jonny then reached in the trashcan and grabbed the bag and began dumping it at the feet of the Venetian security. He did that to the four trashcans on the path to the Strip, he also kicked over six ashtrays on his way.

"I can't believe I'm getting kicked out of this shitty ass place for defending myself against a bitch ass security guard. Fuck that! I'm not going any fucking where. You purple jacket wearing motherfuckers, fuck you fuck niggers, looking like a bunch of grapes, shaped like them too."

"Las Vegas Police Department please come in," the only member of the Venetian security team with a headset said into a Walkie. "We have a disturbance near the south entrance and we need urgent assistance. Thank you."

"Copy that. On the way."

"Purple Coats are some bitches! Why do you have jobs? Your jobs should be eliminated! You fucking clowns don't do a goddamn thing."

"Sir, I suggest you shut the fuck up and get the hell out of here. You don't want to ruin your vacation."

"Who the fuck you talking to like that? Ruin my vacation? Your life is ruined? I'm having fun right now and you're working for a shitty ass apartment and Cup 'o Noodles in a desolate city. You must be fucking insane you Purple bitch. How do you know I'm not from Las Vegas? Oh yeah, because I smell good. This town stinks and is filled with worthless culture absent burnouts. And I bet you were born here fuck nigger. This is your fucking job. Watching niggers like me get at fine ass females and have the time of their life. I'm having the time of my life right now; making you motherfuckers actually do something. "

Jonny pushed the security guard who called the police and as soon as Jonny was getting ready to throw a punch six other Venetian security guards and their purple jackets came to the defense of their manager like a pack of wolves charged to protect the alpha.

Jonny then dropped his guard and walked through the grass, jumped over the fence and onto the sidewalk.

"Fuck you motherfuckers. I don't have time for this shit."

As Jonny began to walk towards Caesar's Palace a Las Vegas Policed Department squad car and three bicycle cops surrounded him. The squad car blocked the far right lane, causing a small back up of cars, which had to merge into the middle lane to continue south on the Strip. Most of the passers by were taxicabs taking drunken partygoers to places where they can get even drunker or where they can get fucked.

It was now three in the morning and Jonny still hadn't received a call or text from any of his friends. But he wouldn't have known anyway because he was still entwined in a battle with Venetian security and now the LVPD.

"What's going on here? Sir, they've asked you to leave the property, so please leave the property of the Venetian Hotel peacefully."

"I'm off their fucking property. They don't own the fucking sidewalk. I've already left."

"Sir, you're still on their property."

"What? These niggers own the sidewalk too? What about the street? Do they own the street?"

Jonny then sprinted to the middle lane of Las Vegas Boulevard and shouted to into the stale desert air "You hear that shitty tax payers of Las Vegas? The sidewalk is property of the Venetian hotel… Am I off of their property now? I'm off their fucking property now, aren't I? Or do these fake Italian motherfuckers own the goddamn street too?"

A pedestrian crossing the crosswalk yelled to Jonny, "Get the fuck out of the street you dumb fuck! Take your drunk ass home!"

"You wouldn't be saying shit if these asshole cops weren't here. Look at your sandals fuck nigger. Shut the fuck up before I knock your ass out. Keep walking."

"Hold on sir, was that threat?" asked one of the eager bicycle cops projecting over the horns of the even more anxious taxicabs.

"That motherfucker didn't have to say shit. Fuck that shit! I'm just performing for you clowns huh? I'm just another shitty ass performer, performing on the shitty ass Las Vegas strip aren't I?"

Jonny then bowed towards the officers and security guards incessantly, over and over again like he was being bated to do an encore. Then Jonny just stood straight up with his hands spread, eyes closed looking towards the blackened Nevada sky, seemingly absorbing the night like the sun when it rises. He stood there until his meditation was interrupted by one of the bicycle officers who asked him, "Do you think you're God or something?"

Jonny snapped immediately out of his self-indulgent trance, he looked at one of the cops who stood outside of the squad car, "Did you give him permission to speak? How long did it take you to get off of the bike? Fuck niggers."

Jonny then walked off towards Caesar's Palace, ensuring that he wasn't being watched or followed before he went up to the hotel room, laid on the bed, and passed out. Darcie called but Jonny couldn't answer.

...

As Jonny relished in his surprise rendezvoused with Darcie and scuffled with Las Vegas Police and Venetian security, Tony was in a VIP booth with Will who was still very jittery and unglued. His speech was erratic and his words began to push up against one another like people rushing out of a burning building in a single file line. Still, he was well dressed; he sweated through his white blouse that was two buttons away from choking him, his grey blazer was soaked like he had walked through a car wash. Will had just ordered three Jäger Bombs, one for Tony and two for himself.

"Where's this bitch at with my motherfucking drinks? There are bitches everywhere in here. I'm getting one of them. Fuck that, all of them and I'm about to have a big ass orgy with all these hoes and none of you fuck niggers are invited. You ain't shit Tony, fuck nigger. I'll get all these bitches... I ain't leaving a single ugly fat bitch for you or Turner, any of them other niggers."

"You're drunk."

The waitress approached the VIP booth with a puzzled looked on her face and their drinks, Will paid the brunette, tipped her two hundred dollars, then smacked her ass with the brutishness of the patriarchy, "Thanks bitch... hurry the fuck up Tony you motherfucking bitch ass nigger. We have to get on these bitches. I might try to get at that waitress. Fuck that. I'm taking these without out you."

Will took both Jäger Bombs like an armored tank; he then stood up from the table and disappeared onto the dance floor before Tony raised his glass to his lips, "That nigger is on some other shit right now," Tony whispered to himself before he took his. He then sat his empty glass on the table and noticed that there was a half-empty bottle of Grey Goose Vodka with two slim pitchers of orange juice and two more filled with cranberry juice surrounded by empty but obviously used drinking glasses. Will had commanded much of his attention and he failed to notice the scene earlier. "This nigger Will must have been going super hard with some other motherfuckers. Whose jacket is this? Whose purse? Am I sitting on someone's sweater?"

Just then a group of four security guards approached the booth. Excuse me sir," politely but patronizingly, said one of the security guards. "This isn't your booth sir, these patrons paid ten thousand dollars and you're trespassing. Come with us," the security guard said as he acknowledged the table's disheveled renters behind him. "Wait motherfuckers... what? What the fuck are you clowns talking about? This is my friend's booth."

"Sadly, you're mistaken," said one of the security guards who was about six feet six and three hundred fifty pounds and could only be distinguished from the others by the large "LV" tattoo in the center of his throat.

"Get up and come with us, let's go, right fucking now asshole."

"You getting loud? Damn nigger, you got hostile real quick."

The only two members of Tao security who spoke then grabbed Tony, they lifted him out of the booth with little resistance. Tony was still attempting to process what was happening to him. The group that had spent ten thousand dollars then reclaimed the table.

Near the bar where Tony and his friends had celebrated earlier was an unlabeled and unnoticeable door that he had been led through by the security guards. The door led to a brightly lit hallway that housed Tao's security office as well as the monitors that displayed images from the closed circuit security cameras located all over the grandiose establishment.

"What were you doing in that booth? You know we can have you arrested for theft?"

Tony looked at the security guards with comedic disbelief.

"What the fuck are you motherfuckers talking about? I was just sitting there. I thought that was my friend's booth.

Why didn't your shitty ass waitress tell us not to sit there? She served us drinks and everything. Fire her!"

"She thought that you guys were with the group but then the group that purchased the table approached us and told us that there were two people sitting in their booth. One of the women left her purse in the booth and it contained over six thousand dollars. She said she saw you going through it. You better hope she has every last penny."

"Are you clowns fucking kidding me? I didn't touch that bitch's purse. This is a big ass misunderstanding. Let me back in this fucking club. You motherfuckers are tripping."

Tony then attempted to open the door and walk back into the club but was grabbed by the security guard who was obviously proud to be from Las Vegas.

"You aren't going anywhere."

Tony laughed, "You're a joke! Don't put your fucking hands on me again. You're hella proud to be from this shitty ass city huh? I come here to have fun. You live and work here. You're losing in life, losing! Off yourself. Let life go. Your life is over!"

Whilst laughing Tony began to dance the tango without a partner in the middle of what had become six security guards, singing a made up tune in-between laughs,

"You guys ain't shit though. Ya'll fuck niggers believe that hoe? It's a goddamn shame. Simple and fucking plain, that accusation is fake, bitch! Check the fucking tape, bitch. Check that fucking tape, though, check the fucking tape. Check that fucking tape though, check the fucking tape."

Tao security, at the behest of Tony's impromptu performance checked their security tapes then allowed him back into the club. They discovered that Tony never touched or reached for any of the purses or jackets, he never rummaged through them. All he had done was have a Jäger Bomb in the VIP booth that unbeknownst to Tony, Will had commandeered.

Back amongst the crowd, Tony attempted to contact Jonny, Malik, and Turner but none of them would respond to his text messages. He sent a text to both David and Mark as well who both responded,

"Busy. Hit you back in a bit. ;)"

It was still early in the night and Tony decided to search the expansive disco for his drunken friends but they couldn't be found.

Tony imagined it being like searching for Osama bin Laden in the rugged Afghanistan terrain, he looked under tables like caves and through the crowd like poppy plants, "These niggers have to be in a cave somewhere. Why can't I find these fuckers?"

He soon found himself, again, on the roof at the bar nearest to the swimming pool. He ordered a vodka tonic that he sipped at the bar as enjoyed the club's scenery.

An amalgamation of cologne and perfume, the preponderance of every kind of alcohol, and the pheromones of men and women desperate for the elation and desire of a Las Vegas one-night stand stained the air. Tony inhaled it all with bored breaths, like the vodka tonic.

Tony grew more restless, fatigued from his search he turned to the bartender to order another round, just before he decided to head back to the hotel and end the night a stunning woman in a seducing red dress interrupted his order. Her cocoa brown hair flowed over down her back like a waterfall. The red dress framed her body; accentuating every feature she wanted it to like a painter emphasizes their subject's most exceptional assets, like a great photographer's lens.

"I'll take whatever he's having," the woman said.

"Hold up! Do I know you?" Tony said then he recognized who she was.

"Your name is Taylor, right? Oh shit! Taylor! How are you doing? Where are the rest of your friends?"

"I can't believe you remembered my name. We didn't really get a chance to talk earlier today. You were too busy with Kristen."

"I'm good with names… and beautiful faces. Are you here with Kristen and all of your other friends?"

"Yeah we came here together but I can't find any of them. They're not at our table. Darcie texted me earlier and told me that she was leaving with your friend Jonny. I don't know where the other girls are though. I waited at our table for over an hour and they just never returned. This place is too fucking huge!"

"I know! I've been trying to find all of my friends too and it is in-fucking-possible in this goddamn metropolis. I think I'm about to leave. It isn't that much fun if you're not with your friends. We're here all weekend. We need to learn to stick together."

"Same with us. We come to the club to escape and enjoy each other's company but that eventually turns into a lot of different agendas then we separate."

"That's what happened to us… I think. We kind of just lost each other. I guess we thought this club was going to be like a club back home in Seattle where you can take a lap or two and find who you came with. This is what always happens to us when we go to clubs though."

Taylor laughed as Tony continued, "This club had to have been an airplane hangar or something at some fucking point, a huge four-story airplane hangar."

The bartender served their drinks.

"Here's to discovery."

"Discovery!"

Then their glasses clinked.

"How has your trip been so far? What did you ladies do after we met in the mall this afternoon?"

"Well, we just went to dinner at this fantastic restaurant in the Bellagio. I forgot the name of it…but it was Italian food, I had the Chicken Parmesan and a salad. It was so delicious. Then we just hung around the Bellagio casino at the craps table. I don't play but this one guy helped me win three hundred dollars. He was on fire… but he was a pig. I think he and his friend were waiting for some girls who were staying there. They were talking so loudly."

"That's funny… They were going hard, besides that, we are in Vegas. A lot of the people come here to get rich and drunk. Most people come to get rich, drunk, and to fuck."

"Those are noble goals I guess," Taylor snickered, "I bet Jonny and Darcie are having a lot of fucking fun right now."

"They're definitely having a lot of fucking fun. They have to be. Jonny is usually pretty good about responding to text messages… fuck all of that though; I'm kind of hungry. You want to go get something to eat? Being abandoned by my friends, taking all of those laps around this humongous club, and you talking about that Italian food has made me hungry as fuck. I need to get some food inside of me before I collapse."

"Oh my God, I'm starving too! Let's go to In & Out. I'm craving a Double Double badly. We can take a cab there. It isn't too far away it's right by UNLV."

"Hell yeah! Jonny lives in Los Angeles so when we visit him or visit our friend Turner in San Diego we always hit up In & Out. I hate their fries though. How well do you know Las Vegas? You're not from here, are you?"

"No, I'm not, there is no way in hell that I could live here. I'm originally from Anaheim in Orange County, SoCal born and raised. The drive is nice and I like guilt free sinning so I come here as often as I can. So I know the city fairly well."

"There is something different about this city. I've been a few times already. Come here for three days and need three weeks to recover once I get back to Seattle and that isn't just because I get fucking wasted. I have to stop by a museum or something and experience some culture, some art, some something that this city is missing... bartender please another round and then I'd like to close out, thank you. It's a cultural wasteland or maybe I just don't know the city well enough..."

"Bartender before you go, can we have two double shots of Patrón? I'll pay with cash... Sinning is easier drunk off your ass. And yeah I've tried to explore this place and get to know it away from the Strip. I think you're accurate. This place has the charm of a three leaf clover."

Taylor and Tony enjoyed their final drinks in Tao. On the way out Tony grabbed a half empty bottle of Belvedere from a VIP booth. They descended the Venetian steps to Las Vegas Boulevard where they hailed the cab that would take them to In & Out Burger.

Two Double Doubles, a chocolate shake for Taylor, strawberry for Tony, both mixed with vodka, and a shared Animal Style fries later the two of them were outside of the Aria Hotel where Taylor was staying. The two were attracted to one another but both were too timid to make the first aggressive move that ensured that the other felt the same, that would animate the obvious attraction. It seemed as if the confidence typically afforded to those drowned in alcohol had been too expensive.

Still, the awkward pair refused to part ways. Their friends still hadn't contacted them so they were beholden to each other to avoid the vacuity and loneliness that could swarm in a city whose bright neon lights still miss the sins hidden by shadows.

"Thanks for riding back to my hotel with me and for the food. Don't their fries taste much better Animal Style?"

"They do, that was too fucking good. Definitely, hit the spot."

Without any hesitation or ambiguity Taylor asked, "Do you want to come up to my room? They have a 24-hour Starbucks in the hotel; we can grab a cup of coffee then head upstairs. I have half a bottle of Jack Daniels… I hope I'm not being too forward or crass. I'm sorry Tony."

"You're crazy Taylor, you're fine. I would love to spend some more time with you. Let's go get some coffee and I am definitely down for another drink… I can't believe none of our asshole friends have said anything to us. They must be having the time of their goddamn lives, fucking fuckers. But fuck them; that's exactly what I'm having. You saved my night."

"I feel that way too. That's why it isn't close to being over yet. More fun is to be had."

Taylor's hotel room was actually a large suite littered with clothes and suitcases, cups and empty beer and spirit bottles. The discarded pair drank their coffee with Jack Daniels.

"Did you and all of your girlfriend's get a room together? There are only three suitcases."

"You are very attentive… and no Darcie is fucking Jonny at Caesar's Palace. Her and Kristen are sharing a room there and Kim, Karen and I booked here. Darcie is insane!

The last time we shared a room with her we all had to split the damage she caused, two thousand fucking dollars six ways. It was fucking ridiculous. I love that girl but she has mental issues. Hotel windows in Vegas only open six inches wide because of her."

"I would have made her ass pay for everything. Fuck that shit!"

"That's my girl. Shit, we had a lot of fucking fun that weekend. The story is that much greater because of her madness. I'm just saying… she's one crazy ass bitch."

"Maybe that's why her and Jonny were so attracted to one another. She may have met her perfect match."

"That's kind of scary to think about, if Jonny is anything like Darcie that's like two torrential hurricanes of desert dust ascending onto Vegas at once… we better take cover."

A brief but coy and torturous silence proceeded Taylor's poetic pronouncement. A silence broken by something they both wanted. With a romantics shy uncertainty Tony asked, "Can I give you a…" before he was able to finish Taylor had her hands on his cheeks and her tongue down his throat, kissing him incessantly, wildly, and with the vigor of years without human contact, the passion of sexual repression.

"I… thought… you'd… never… make… a… move." Each word Taylor spoke a release between kisses she had wanted since she saw Tony at the bar. Tony eagerly reciprocated Taylor's impossibly equivocated fervor as his hands found their way from her face down to her neck and breasts. They then grabbed her slim waist and then her tight ass. Taylor pulled Tony up from the chair his belt buckle in one hand, the almost empty bottle of Jack Daniels in the other, and led him to the bed. Tony pushed her onto it and continued to act upon the answer to his unfinished question and to seek the questions already answered. Taylor fell back onto the bed and finished the bottle of Jack Daniel's throwing it and her dress onto the scorching carpet.

He moved from her lips to her neck slow like water from a sun-drenched iceberg, his lips creating musical moans that made her body sing like a siren and shiver like the arctic. Tony went from her neck to her shoulders to all of the sensuality that his hands already knew.

Tony took off his shirt as Taylor took his pants; Taylor's dress and now her bra were with a pile of clothes and empty bottle of Jack Daniel's on the side of the bed.

They were still in the midst of the nature their timid minds had quashed when Darcie came through the suite door enraged. Tony and Taylor attempted to continue their discovery but couldn't ignore Darcie's mammoth screams.

"Faggot! He must be a fucking faggot! Why else would he be ignoring me? Why else would he fucking leave me hanging like that! ME! That dumb ass faggot motherfucker, bitch ass nigger! Fuck Jonny! Fuck him in his stupid fucking ass!"

"Darcie! What the fuck are you doing here? Go back to your own room!"

"Is Jonny in here? One of you bitches better not be fucking him! Where the fuck is he?"

"He isn't fucking here! Get the fuck out of here Darcie! You dumb fucking bitch!"

Darcie had in her hand a bottle of Glenlivet 15 Year just opened.

"He didn't want to fuck me? He wanted to go fuck some Vegas sissy? Fuck that faggot!"

Darcie then engulfed as much of the Glenlivet as she could and flung the rest of bottle across the room and through the room's sixty-inch flat screen television, then to her knees she fell and she began to sob like a child who had just lost a puppy.

"What the fuck is wrong with him? I had my mind on him all fucking night. He wanted me. I know he did. Why doesn't he want me anymore?"

Taylor, naked, but with a nurse's response went to console her whimpering friend, weak from rage.

"I just wanted to fuck him Taylor. He is nothing special at all, but I had to fuck him. I just had to."

Tony sat on the edge of the bed of disappointing outcomes amazed at the unsteadiness of emotion only confined by the size of the suite. If the suite had been a floor or two below the Aria's foundation would have surely quaked.

Tony never took his eyes off of the two women huddled by embrace as he put on his pants, shirt, and shoes. Tony kissed Taylor on the top of her head as he left the suite and whispered into her ear free from the top of Darcie's head, "I'll be in town all weekend."

...

Turner lie on the floor of the Venetian's lobby he shouted with every rowdy breath in his inebriated body, "Remove me from these fucking premises! I ain't going nowhere! You motherfuckers ain't shit! Force me to leave this shitty place!"

When security approached his seemingly comatose body, still like a protesting monk who spouts ignorant axioms, Turner jumped up and ran away holding a glass of "Turn Up" in his right hand, "Y'all wanna race, you fat motherfuckers? You'll never catch me! I can do this all night. You lazy fucks are already tired? You," Turner said pointing at Venetian security whilst running, "…aren't shit! Look, you

Grimace looking fat motherfucker; let's race, if you beat me I'll leave quietly. I'll leave peacefully."

Turner paused and stood as he was in the blocks for the four hundred meter dash. Five more security guards then came into the lobby to try and subdue the drunkard with uncanny agility, balance, and quickness for his current state. He could most likely pass any sobriety test, if the officer's Breathalyzer was broken.

"None of y'all can catch me. I'll go back into Tao right fucking now. And y'all wouldn't be able to do shit about it!"

Turner then sprinted back to Tao's entrance. He hurdled three velvet ropes and halted in front of the hostess' podium, where he laid back onto the Venetian's marble floor and continued his absurd protest, "I ain't going anywhere! What the fuck y'all Purple Coats going to do? You can't catch me, give up and go back to watching cameras. Go drink your coffee and eat your muffins and bullshit and watch the motherfucking cameras."

Turner again hopped up and hurdled the three velvet ropes in front of Tao, from one rope to the other like hopscotch, back and forth three times before he ran back to the center of the Venetian's main lobby and laid down, his back once more on the brumal marble, he espoused, "I told y'all! Y'all aren't shit! You... all... are... not... shit! How much y'all making and you can't catch me? That's probably why you're not making more. Do your motherfucking job and catch me! Kick me out! You could never work for me. I want the Venetian's management front and center! Fire these fucking clowns! You have to work harder or you'll be wearing those shitty purple coats for life. Probably, been wearing it for half of your pathetic fucking Las Vegas lives already."

Turner was back on his feet, he smirked as he put the glass of 'Turn Up' to his lips.

After every last drop his tongue tasted he threw the glass up in the air, it almost reached the high mounted crystal chandelier about thirty feet from the top of Turner's six foot four frame and before glass shards littered the lobby's floor Turner had already ran out the hotel's doors and into a taxicab.

"Where the fuck are these clowns at? I can't believe they would just leave and not let me know a goddamn thing. This is some bullshit!" The cab driver unnerved by Turner's frayed disposition, "Where to sir?"

"To Drais, I don't know what hotel it's in. It's your job to know though. If you don't know, I'm not paying you shit."

"Bally's it is."

"Good."

The line to get into Drais disheartened Turner who refused to stand alone in line and portray obvious desperation. He walked from the back of the line to the front and to the back of the line again in search of a woman to keep him company. He had gotten a few advances and phone numbers at Tao but by the time he could take advantage of his hard worked flirting he was in the lobby at Bally's looking for another connection to appease his immense sexual satiety, his desire for amusement unabated.

Turner's attempts to poach a woman from the line were futile as afterhours consisted of couples that hooked up earlier in the evening at one of the many nightclubs on the Strip. He only met shoulder shrugs and intense disinterest and sinister stares from the men who knew he was trying to poach their catch. The task became too daunting so he walked into the Bally's Sports Book to watch the highlights of the opening day of the NCAA Tournament and to conclude his night with some food and a martini. On the largest television screen were the highlights from the Illinois game that had ruined his parlay earlier in the day.

"Illinois is trash! Fuck them!" Turner said under his breath as he sought a waitress to take his food and drink order. A waitress soon approached him; Turner had his hand raised like he had the answer to the professor's question, "Can I have the steak and eggs, eggs scrambled hard, steak well medium well and a dirty vodka martini please?"

"Anything else, Hun?"

"I would also like to order you sitting down and having a drink with me."

The waitress was flattered; she sincerely giggled then said, "I can't do that, but I'll have your drink and food order right away, handsome."

For an hour Turner sat in the Sports Book and ate his steak and eggs, ceaselessly he threw advances at the waitress who knew how to bait a larger tip, Turner wasn't oblivious he purposely enticed her flirts. The Illinois loss that cost him a cheaper vacation the background to his chewing.

Unbeknownst to Turner he was being ogled from the other end of the Sports Book. A woman, suspiciously alone, had watched Turner's every move. From the time he exited the cab to his hunt of the Drais' line she was interested in what he was determined to find. She knew that he had been in search of a beautiful woman to end his night with and she was intrigued by his determination, and determined herself to be that woman.

Turner asked for the check and when he went to retrieve his wallet he realized that he still had the flask that Jonny had given him earlier in the night, it was half empty. He drank from it like a lost canteen full of water found in an expansive desert. She returned with his receipt and an amorous smile. Curiously, a phone number had been handwritten on the top of his receipt next to the waitress' printed name, Lisa, at the bottom near the subtotal was a kiss in red lipstick with a note "call me." Lisa wasn't wearing lipstick.

The check was paid in cash and Turner left a forty percent gratuity. Without thought and with the haste of a junky with a hard hustled twenty dollars he called the number on the receipt, phone to his ear he watched Lisa who was behind the bar. The phone rang and rang and eventually went to an automated answering machine that only read back to him the number he called. Suddenly, he felt a kiss on his ear, then the soft breath and even sweeter sound of a woman's voice, "Don't leave a message, I never check my voicemail."

The woman startled Turner, "What the fuck? You're just going to run up on a nig..." he jumped out of his chair and nearly knocked over the table that was still littered with dishes. He paused once his eyes distinguished the beauty of the woman who went through the trouble of getting her phone number onto his receipt. The woman then chuckled, "I didn't mean to startle you. I noticed that you were looking for someone... or something earlier. I thought it might have been me."

Turner adapted to the game the beautiful stranger had played effortlessly, "Finally, I found who I was looking for. I probably would have found you sooner if I knew your name. I could have asked one of these shitty casino workers if they knew you," he had also subdued his disbelief.

"Denise, my name is Denise. You weren't looking too hard. All those girls you tried to talk to were taken. I've been here by myself and you didn't even notice. But here I am."

"I'm Turner... I'm sorry Denise. I don't know how I could have missed you. I tried to describe you to everyone in the casino but they didn't know you, they hadn't seen a beautiful five feet six inches tall woman with wondrous curly hair and a fucking ass so fat that it makes a nigger want to elope. I was so worried about you."

"Actually, I think I was more worried about you. I'm disappointed that you weren't looking more diligently because I was watching you and waiting for you to acknowledge me... but it's all the same. I'm still going to get what I want."

"I felt like I was very meticulous I was so thorough I worked up an appetite. It's tiresome looking for someone who you've never met; still I'm glad that I'm here staring at your intoxicating brown eyes. How about you? Are you hungry? I know you're hungry and thirsty after your expansive search. You want to at least grab a drink? We can go sit at the bar."

"Didn't you just eat? I don't think the waitress you were flirting with will appreciate you giving me her attention. You want to grab a drink here? Let's go somewhere else. I know you know of a greater place than this. I know of a place right off the Strip."

"I don't give a fuck about her. Let's just grab a drink here. Don't act like you aren't going to drink because you care what the waitress thinks."

"I'm not. I approached you, didn't I? Just thought you made more progress than it looked like you were making. I don't want to fuck up your game. She may fuck you once she's off of work... what time is it right now, three in the morning, three thirty? She probably gets off at eight. I can leave and you can wait. And that great place off of the Strip is your hotel room."

"You must have been watching me on some stalker shit. I was just having fun. I know she was just trying to get a larger tip but she enjoyed it and so did I. I have the money and she needs it. My hotel room is the perfect place to have a drink and it's actually right on the Strip. The bar is always open there."

"You should have just gone to a strip club."

"I wouldn't eat steak and eggs at a strip club... and maybe that's where I was going next before you found me, you don't know shit."

"Wow, you're bold with beautiful women."

"Look, you came up to me. What's going on right now? What do you want me to say? You're the one just trying to make conversation, you obviously know what I want and I know what the fuck you want. You approached me, kisses on the receipt and everything."

"What you think I want is what I need. Are we going to your hotel room or what? And you better fuck the shit out of me..."

"If that's all you want with me, I'll happily oblige. That's what I was looking to do. You sought me out and caught me, great fucking catch."

"I'll be the judge of that. Don't make me throw you back nigger."

Turner and Denise then leave the Sports Book and walk through Bally's slot machine littered lobby both observing and mocking all of the men who haunted the line into Drais like Turner had done a couple of hours earlier. They both pointed and laughed at all of the men who couldn't find what they wanted at Marquee, Pure, Tao or any other nightclub in the city. They felt sorry for all of the lonely women, so lonely that desperation, and Turner, wouldn't notice them. Attracting a beautiful woman for coitus seemed profoundly laborious in a city that promised at least that. Luckily, Turner had been gifted with the power, unknown by him, to attract lonely beautiful women, the evidence Denise's presence.

"I was doing what these clowns are doing an hour and a half ago. I'm fucking tonight though, aren't I Denise? So I win, victory is mine!"

Denise laughed then clutched Turner's arm tighter as they walked towards their sexual fantasies until suddenly Turner was pushed to the ground. A man about ten inches shorter than Turner's six feet four inches frame had pushed him in the back. The man claimed Denise as his territory similarly to Mexico after the Louisiana Purchase, which he made sure everyone understood as evident by his belligerence and deafening screams.

"Who the fuck are you? You better leave my bitch alone before I fuck you up! You preppy ass fuck nigger… Denise, how you fucking with this nigger right here? Let's go back to our room right now. You're obviously drunk. How the fuck are you going to step out on me like this you dumb ass bitch?"

Denise didn't respond. She nurtured Turner who was still in shock and had no clue why he was being challenged. He just knew that he was on the ground; he also knew that he had to defend himself. Denise relished in the vexation blooming in Turner's eyes. The petulance that the short man had caused brought about a rage in him that had briefly erased his chief goal for the evening.

Turner picked himself up off of Bally's stained teal blue carpet and furiously with the immediacy of a pregnant woman whose water just broke, approached the much smaller man, "What the fuck is up you midget motherfucker? I'm going to pretend that you pushing me was a fucking accident. I don't want to have to destroy you in here and plus I don't want to get locked up for child abuse. Your girl chose me. She chose up. You lose… take this fucking loss like a motherfucking man you short bitch… your girl is taller than you. She doesn't respect you."

"Fuck you! That's my bitch! You aren't leaving here with her," yelled the small man.

"Fuck you Spencer! Your little ass doesn't know how to treat me or satisfy me. Where the fuck have you been for four hours? Stuck on the toilet, your legs swinging? Do you need your ass wiped again? I need someone who can see over the average bar counter you little fucking asshole."

"Fuck you Denise, you drunk ass bitch, you fucking slut! And fuck this tall ass nigger too! I'll still beat his motherfucking ass! Then I'm going to beat your motherfucking ass for stepping out on me like this, embarrassing me and shit."

An angry Spencer in a siege to reclaim his occupied territory, took off his gold chain and swung it at Turner. This caused a three-inch vertical gash on Turner's forehead that ran from the beginning of his hairline to the top of his left eyebrow. The wound bled profusely.

"How the fuck you going to act like this on the day we get engaged? You dumb bitch! My homies told me that you were a slut; you did fuck that nigger Michael didn't you? And I didn't listen. I should have known those rumors going around our high school were fucking true. You're a hoe and it's undeniable. I was out getting our hotel room ready for a romantic evening and you're out here with this tall ass fuck nigger. I knew you always liked tall niggers. Fuck you bitch! Your trick and I, we're going to war."

Blood had dripped from the newly acquired wound down Turner's forehead onto the clothes he had bought earlier in the day. The shock from the blow and the situation quickly subsided as he rushed his assailant like a bull after a particularly irritating and ridiculing matador and his red cape.

"You fucked up!" Turner said as he tackled the unforeseen pest. Once on top of his bane he began to throw punches all with his right arm and fist like a chain and wrecking ball, which pummeled the newly engaged miniature man. Both of their blood joining the beer soaked carpet.

"Yeah! What's up now? You dumb motherfucker! You might be Napolean but this is the Battle of Waterloo. You fucked up your entire night, you should have set up those flowers and candles around a gurney you dumb short fuck! Now... I'm... going... to fuck... your fiancé! Nice... and... mother... fucking... slow," Turner paused, he remained atop the unexpected and remaining obstacle in obtaining his original goal of coitus, "Think about that as your wounds heal, you little ass bitch."

Turner dismounted the now bloody short man who writhed in immense pain on the casino floor. He then grabbed Denise's hand in his, blood soaked and swelling, and they exited Bally's, got into a cab right away, and just as swiftly as they entered the cab they arrived at Caesar's Palace.

Jonny was sleep fully dressed on the queen-sized bed that he was supposed to share with Turner. No one had any particular claim to the room as they each paid an equal share in booking it. Jonny laid on his back his arms shading his eyes from the rising sun, which had chased away the darkness and peered through the hotel rooms white sheer curtains.

"Jonny! Jonny! Wake your motherfucking ass up and get the fuck out!" Turner yelled from the hotel room's doorway. Denise's face looked as if she had thought Turner's orders. And without a word or an acknowledgement of their presence, Jonny awoke and left the hotel room.

"Good looking out bro," Turner said as Jonny entered the hallway and the door closed abruptly behind him.

...

"No!" yelled Malik loudly. It echoed through the bathroom like a scream at the bottom of a scopic canyon. It was a quick affirmation, a realization that he had missed whatever had happened that night.

Malik somberly exited the men's bathroom located in hallway to the right of Tao's entrance. Disoriented and depressed by his surroundings, he walked out of the Venetian hotel. The sun, on its way up to the sky, had blinded him. He used his right arm to block out its streaming rays as he checked his phone and returned his last missed call.

"Jonny, man. Where the fuck are you?"
"Nigger, where are you? Where the fuck have you been all night? I blew your phone the fuck up!" Jonny said angrily but with sincere concern.

"You in the room? I'm on my way to the roulette table. Come downstairs. I'll be at table twenty four," relayed Malik.

Jonny's six feet three inches frame stretched as he hung up the phone. His feet and hands reached across hallway floor from one wall to the other. He lay outside of their hotel room so that Turner could consummate the first day of the trip. He shook off his alcohol induced coma and eventually gathered the strength he needed to pick himself up and head downstairs to the roulette table twenty four where Malik held a rum and coke in one hand and was pounding on the table rooting for the small white marble to land on any black number, with the other, "Let's go! You better hit you fucking piece of shit, you better fucking hit... Fuck... Fuck this cheating ass game. Dealer you're fucking cheating I know you are. Where are the magnets? Turn off the magnets."

Malik then turned his frustration onto the other patrons at the table. He taunted, "You aren't gonna hit shit! You're hella weak at this bull shit ass game." He sat out the latest spin because he was digging in his wallet for cash to buy more chips. His wallet was empty and for a brief moment he remembered that Will owed him four hundred forty dollars, "Bitch ass nigger Will left me broke down here," then he remembered that Jonny and Tony gave him five hundred dollars, which he had in his left sock. He took out the money and as he exchanged the money for chips he acknowledged a gambler who seemed to have exceptional luck, "Oh shit! You're pretty good. How do you play? Your putting chips on almost all of these fucking numbers right here. Why? Tell me right now," he demanded of the patron in a grey, tailored, three-piece suit that had just won two thousand dollars.

"Show me how the fuck you're doing this. I'm trying to learn. I'm coming up off of you tonight," Malik denied the sun's presence. The patron seemed more than willing to share his knowledge of the game with the worst gambling odds in Las Vegas with an unapologetically brash individual who was desperate to win big so he could salvage the night he was still living.

Casino security and management approached Malik about his behavior, mainly the banging on the roulette table, Malik responded to their concern, "Unless you're here to get me another drink leave me the fuck alone. I'm having fun. Let me spend my money." Security and management had let Malik and his antics prevail because the casino was nearly empty and he had just purchased five hundred dollars in chips.

Jonny made it down stairs and approached Malik who had just won three hundred dollars using the strategy of the well-dressed man who Malik discovered was from Houston and was in Las Vegas for a night before he flew to Atlantic City.

"Where the hell were you? Seriously, I was trying to hit you up. I hit up everyone… I just assumed you found some pussy and were preoccupied, I know that had to have been the case."

"I didn't find shit, bro, no pussy…" then Malik addressed his roulette sage of chance, "Look, I'm about to put my chips wherever you put them and you aren't gonna say shit about it..." then sullenly to Jonny, "I just randomly woke up in the bathroom, sitting on the toilet. I think I had to take a shit while I was in Tao. I hate taking shits inside clubs so I left and used one in the Venetian. I guess I just fucking passed out... Yes! I'm coming up... I was way more wasted than I thought. My head was in my lap, drooling and shit, what a shitty fucking night. What the fuck happened with y'all?"

"I don't have a fucking clue what happened to them other niggers, all I know is that my night was fucking trash as well. Last thing I remember is Turner kicking me out of the hotel room. At least he had a great time. As a matter of fact call one of them niggers. See what's good and if they're trying to go get breakfast right now, call the waitress over too. Order a whiskey sour and give it to me."

Malik pulled out his phone and he had a picture text messages from a sender denoted in his phone as 'Tao Chick.' He had his arms around her as they had taken several selfies together. Before he attempted to get into contact with Tony he looked through his photos to see what pictures, if any, he had taken.

After a few swipes across his phone's screen Malik burst out laughing, an uncontrollable breath stealing laugh, the kind of laugh that gives headaches. He was oblivious to the fact that he had just won another one hundred and fifty dollars.

"Who is this random ass redhead chick? I took a ton of pictures with her." Malik then showed Jonny a picture of him embraced with a redheaded woman wearing a dark red dress. Malik swiped across the screen a few more times as Jonny looked on.

"Oh shit! I did get some pussy my nigger, look!" Malik appeared to be in a stairwell he had the redheaded woman pinned against a wall, her back to the camera, she taunted him, "Fuck me harder, you asshole, fuck me!"

"I don't remember any of this shit my nigger. Oh my God, I'm dead right now!" Malik could not contain his laughter, his face flush and his eyes swelled with tears. He pounded on the roulette table harder and harder as those tears ran down his cheeks.

"This is comedic gold... what the fuck? I can't believe she let me take this video. I'm definitely hitting her up again. She's looking like a winner. May need a round two... I have hella shit on here my nigger."

"Damn bro, in a stairwell? She was fucking ready for action, you lucky ass bitch. What else do you have on your phone? I'm fucking hating on you right now. I was so close with that girl Darcie but I failed miserably..."

Malik swiped to the left then pressed play on the very next video, it was video of Terrance who had his head down on the rooftop bar in Tao, he was asleep, fatigued from his attempt to catch up to his friends who had been drunk before his plane took flight. In the video Terrance was approached by multiple security guards; what is true in most nightclubs and bars in the United States is also true in Sin City, the city that owns inhibitions, where the pursuit of pleasure is cheered then distributed, you cannot sleep even if sleep is your pleasure.

The security guards attempted to wake Terrance but he was in a Snow White slumber with no Prince in the vicinity. A large security guard lifted the drunkard onto his shoulders and carried him out of the camera's purview.

"Why didn't we say anything?" said Malik, still laughing hysterically.

Then upon the phone's lens came a red headed woman, the same woman from the stairwell; seemingly sorrowful she said, "Isn't that your friend? Why aren't you doing anything?"

Turner then joins the scene, he pushed the red head out of the way, "Fuck them niggers man. I'm about to go help out my boy. Fuck that pig roasting mother... fucking... bitch... ass... motherfucking... mother, mother, motherfucking fake ass cop."

Turner then runs off camera in the direction of the security guard and Terrance to reveal Will having a heart attack.

Malik said monotonically, "I think Will is in the hospital my nigger. I didn't even know he was at Tao."

Jonny responded, "He said he'd be there and there was no way that we were finding him in that monstrous place. But yeah he's in the hospital. That nigger looks like he was tazed or some shit."

The video then goes black not before Will is attended to by some of Tao's patrons. Malik collects his chips, he had won seven hundred sixty dollars, and then he called Tony.

"Tony, where are you?"

"I'm in a cab on my way back to the hotel. What's good? You niggers trying to get breakfast?"

"Yeah... Jonny and me are about to head back to the room right now..." Tony interrupted Malik, "You hear what happened to Will? That nigger is in the hospital. His dumb ass had too many energy drinks. I just got off the phone with Mark, him and David are with him right now they're heading to that Denny's on the southern part of the strip. They didn't even end up going to Marquee. They went too hard earlier with some females from Seattle or something."

"I got partial video of his heart attack on my phone... I was too gone last night. I can't remember shit that happened once we entered the club."

"I'm pulling up to the hotel right now. Don't go to the room yet; wait for me."

Tony, Jonny, and Malik arrived to a room silent except for snores loud like wolves howling at the desert moon or crickets outside the windows of houses mere feet from country meadows.

Jonny, Tony, and Malik entered the room quietly; they tiptoed through the doorway they even insured that the room door did not close noisily. Snores still polluted the silence, which had now been intruded by three giggly breaths.

Tony approached the bed where Turner and Denise laid he nudged Turner, "Turner? Turner? Wake your bitch ass up you fuck nigger. Let's go eat..."

Malik interjected, "Kick this big footed broad out and let's fucking go."

The sun peered through the hotel room's curtains and a single ray illuminated Denise's feet with the fervor of a lit candle in the middle of a large black room. Tony could not help but comment, "Damn Turner, I didn't know you found Sasquatch. This chick wears my size. Tell her to let me borrow some shoes... Will had a heart attack he, Mark and David just left the hospital and they're at Denny's right now. Get the fuck up and let's fucking go."

Denise had been awoken and laughed, "I'll stomp you fuck niggers out though, put my feet up your ass. I got what the fuck I want. Fuck you niggers. I have to go make up with my fiancé anyway."

Tony responded, "You tracked Turner down. I better calm down because if you put your foot in my ass you may stab me in my heart. I don't want you to step all over me. But now you have to get the fuck out! Kick rocks... And I hope you know your fiancé is a fuck nigger, I hope you know that."

Denise as she dressed in front of a snoring Turner and the ridicule of his friends,

"Yep! That's why his bitch ass is my fiancé. Again, fuck you and you and you! I'm out… Turner thanks for the dick, I'm glad that I forced you to meet me."

The hotel room door slammed behind Denise then Turner sat up in the bed like he had been awoken by a fire alarm, "Did I fuck that chick?"

Malik with intense confusion responded, "You tell us, you goddamn clown. Unless you were using these condoms on the floor for water balloons I think you did. Get dressed you Big Foot fucking son of a bitch! Will had a heart attack. Let's get the hell out of here."

Jonny, Turner, Tony, and Malik arrived at Denny's where David, Mark, and Will sat in a large booth. The first words out of Will's mouth whilst he opened another 5 Hour Energy Drink, "What are we doing tonight?"

A Remote Mind

All of these years and she still can't look at me. After all we went through. After everything that happened between us, she can't bring herself to look at me. I wonder what I did to her. I guess I know but fuck it and fuck her.

"Hey! Hey Will, hold up! Will, is that you?"

I hear her voice. I can't believe I am still in love with her. I never could get her off of my mind. Why do I still give a damn about her? Why the fuck do I love her, still? Get out of my fucking head!

"Hey Will. Will, it's me Mary. I know you remember me. How are you? It has been forever since we've seen each other and you can't be more excited than that?"

"I'm sorry Mary. I thought that your voice was in my head. It has been forever, hasn't it?"

"Well, how have you been Willie? You look good. I can't believe you still have that hat. That's why I was certain it was you."

She snickered at me after all of these years; her eyes are still on the top of my head.

"I just can't let it go. It's still my favorite hat. And I'm doing well Mary. I can't complain. How have you been? You still look fucking amazing."

"Watch your mouth Willie. You still have that potty mouth, don't you? What are you up to right now? Let's catch up for a bit. You have a little time don't you?"

I probably should not accept her invitation but I don't have anything significant planned today. I am just out looking for a good cup of coffee. I was just going to go back home and paint. I have time for her.

"Well I was just going to grab a cup of coffee. You can join me if you want."

"That sounds great Willie. I don't have to be back at work until two. Does this café serve food?"

"I know of one that does."

"Ok sweet, Willie. Lead the way."

I can't believe I am walking with her to have coffee and lunch. I can't believe that she works down here. I walk down this street everyday. She's here everyday and we've never ran into each other. The world is really big.

"I didn't know you worked downtown."

Now she's going to tell me where she works. I can't believe I'm going to know where she works.

"I moved downtown about a month ago. I got a job assisting a local designer open up a shop on 6th and Los Angeles. Jonny Castellanos, have you heard of him?"

"I haven't."

"His dresses have been on the runway at the Grammys and the Oscars and many other award shows and events. He wants me to be his assistant designer. I don't know if I should take the position because I am still working on my own line but it is a great opportunity, and he's an amazing artist. I am so confused. His vision is outstanding. The body is his canvas. But he is own artist, you know? I want people to wear me. To understand how I see the body. So I'm going to be running his store. Downtown is a weird place, I am still trying to get used to it. "

It's like we have always been together. This is how she would talk to me when she came home from work, our small studio apartment, what a shitty fucking place. No wonder we're not together. She still has her passion.

"What have you been up to Willie? You still at the same job? Are you still in school?"

"Yes to both. I'm still selling cell phones and I'm now working on my Master's. I finally transferred to UCLA, where I got my bachelors, and I am still there, after all of those years at Los Angeles City College. I have been taking a lot of pictures and I have been painting much more. I am planning an exhibition of my work on Gallery Row.

I have a few artists from all over town supporting the exhibition. Oh, well here's the café. Have you ever been here?"

Hopefully she says no so I can tell her about it and all of the other cool places to eat and drink downtown. Maybe we can be in each other's lives again and at least be friends. I hope I don't talk too much like I always did, do. Damn, she still looks incredible. I bet her pussy still smells so sweet. I think I can smell it. I wonder if I can still get her as wet as I used to. She used to love when I fucked her. I loved fucking her.

"I told you that I am new to downtown. I haven't been anywhere but work and home. Jonny usually cooks so I don't eat out much."

"Oh, I see."

She has a fucking boyfriend and he's in fashion. She doesn't have a problem living with him. He's probably in the closet, faggot.

"This place looks great Willie. The ambiance is welcoming."

"Yeah I come here all the time, usually in the evenings after work or after a long day of painting. They have great coffee and their food is incredible."

"Willie what are you doing getting coffee right now? Do you have another job or something? How many cups have you had today?"

"This is going to be my first cup. I have been painting all morning. I am still getting ready for the exhibition. I want it to be ready in time for the next art walk. I only work three days a week if that. I survive on my art. I can only afford coffee and paint after paying all of my bills."

"I was going to say that you have lost a lot of weight Willie. You need to start eating more. Have you just been painting and drinking coffee all of these years? But congratulations on the exhibition. You've made a lot of progress. You should give me more details about the show and maybe I'll stop by."

She still has a problem with my art. But she is a bit more encouraging. Maybe she is being condescending. She's good at that.

"Yes I have. That's all I ever want to do. And of course, my exhibition is going to be at the old Bang Gallery on 4th and Spring, next Thursday at 8:00PM. I hope I don't die before my first exhibition. That's usually how my life works."

"You still possess that very dark sense humor Willie and I still love it."

"Why is that dark?"

"That's all you want to do? Is drink coffee and paint? You hope you don't die in a week? There is more pleasure in life than that. You can't just be interpreting Willie you have to be doing. You're a fabulous painter and I understand, now, that you'll be a painter your entire life but it's okay to take a break and become inspired. Dream bigger."

I know that she has said these same words to me before. I am essentially an underachiever. She always told me I was underachieving like I didn't know that I was. Like underachieving isn't a choice. I still love that she still cares.

"I am always painting so I am always inspired. I never paint unless inspired. We order here at the counter then we can sit wherever we want. I'll take a cup of coffee. Do you know what you want yet Mary?"

"Yes. I'll have your seasonal fruit bowl with strawberry Greek yogurt and a Blue Moon. Willie it's too late in the day for a cup of coffee. Grab a beer, on me."

"Why thank you Mary Berry. It's too early for a beer. I'll take a shot of Glenlivet 12 year with that coffee black?"

"I haven't heard that name in years. I can see you still like to Irish up your coffee. I guess the good things never change."

I can't tell if she is being condescending again or generally supportive. She is drinking a beer at 12:30PM. It's okay to drink after noon you always adhere to the rules.

"Yeah, liquid inspiration. I have been drinking all morning. Johnnie Walker has a hold on me."

"I know you've been drinking Willie. I can smell it on your breath. You can afford coffee, paint, and whiskey too. You've moved up to Johnny Walker, huh? At least you're not drinking, what was it? Evan Williams? That bottom shelf garbage you used to come home with. That means you're making some money."

She always talked about money even more than she talked about herself or talked down on me. Her faggot boyfriend probably has a lot of it.

"I am surviving the best I can. Let's sit outside. It's a beautiful day."

"It is a beautiful day, isn't it? I am glad I ran into Willie. You changed your phone number so I couldn't get into contact with you but I was wondering if you still had my iPod? I know it's an awkward request after all of this time and you probably pawned it or sold it on Craigslist but it would be nice if you still had it. We have a lot of work to do at the new shop and it would be nice to have my own music to listen to."

She flagged me down for an iPod? This spoiled, high maintenance dumb ass bitch that I love for some dumb ass reason. She saw me and thought of her iPod, only. After a six year relationship that is all I am. I have prevented her from denying the sounds of the world, of the universe. Why hasn't she bought a new one already? She doesn't have an iPhone or some shit? I bought the iPod for her. She didn't want anything from me in the end and now she wants music. I am still glad I am here with her. Anything she wants, still.

"Yeah I still have it. I left it at home today for some reason. I usually have it with me but today I just forgot or didn't think to bring it. I probably wouldn't have heard you calling my name earlier. Good thing I forgot it. Isn't it?"

I wish I had brought it so I didn't have to see her again.

"That would have been convenient Willie. I'm glad that you did forget it though. You wouldn't have heard me, even though I grabbed your shoulder. And we wouldn't be sitting here having this conversation. This is nice."

"Yeah. How is your fruit bowl and yogurt?"

"It's delicious! This place is great. I love that they have a full bar as well. I've had a couple myself this morning. Every hour not drinking isn't worth living."

She always hated my drinking. Now she's an alcoholic stealing my axioms of alcoholism. I need more Glenlivet.

"Another round on me Mary."

"Let's do it!"

I wish she really wanted me to take her to the bathroom of this café and fuck her brains out. Let's do it baby. Let's fucking do it.

"Awesome! Do you want another Blue Moon? Or do you want something else?"

"JC loves Glenlivet too. We drink that and MaCallans all of the time. I'll take a glass of 18 Year Glenlivet neat and another Blue Moon, as well. Thank you Willie."

"Cool. I'll be right back."

I cannot believe that I am here with the love of my life, drinking with her and buying her drinks again. She sucks but I love her. Why did she order an 18 Year and another Blue Moon on me? That's already double what she paid for both of us. She is not my girlfriend anymore. I know I still love her but damn she can still spend my money. She is still worth it.

"Here you go. You drink better than me now."

Maybe a few more and she'll fuck me.

"Well, the student surpasses the teacher sometimes."

And sometimes the teacher fucks the student.

"I can't explain it but our meeting once again reminds me of this old man I always see on the bus. I see this old man everyday on my way to class. An old cantankerous and ornery black man who gets on at the same stop as me, Whittier and Soto. He always stands at the doorway in the rear of the bus shouting at the bus driver. Shaking his cane and his fists, waving his briefcase at the bus driver. No matter how short or long the bus he always stood in the furthermost rear exit, shouting, refusing to adjust the volume in his voice to the size of the bus. To the old man every bus had three doors and six wheels. I rarely heard what he was shouting. Actually, the very first time I noticed the old man was the only time I ever heard him speak. The very first time I saw him, before I placed my headphones over my ears he shouted, 'This nigger can't drive the bus because he's too busy talking to that Mexican nigger. If I was driving this motherfucking bus everybody on this motherfucking bus would be where they had to be.' I always saw him but never heard him after that. I saw how demonstrative he was and could probably replicate his mannerisms but I never heard him. I think most people on the bus just tuned him out, no one aboard the bus reacted to his words not even the bus drivers. No one cared what he had to say or what he did. He was just there, no matter how animated he became, no matter how visibly furious. Thanks to your iPod I never heard anyone or anything but the music. I was estranged from the world, a sullen but necessitated remoteness. I can't wait to hear what else he has to say."

"You can bring the iPod by the shop on 6th and Los Angeles. It's right on the southeast corner. Thank you and thank you for the drinks. I have to get back to work but maybe I'll see you around again soon. I truly do miss your little stories. You should have been a writer, maybe. Take care, Willie."

She still needs something from me. She still loves me.

The Art of Chaos

In the midst of societal upheaval there are those who disrupt.
There are also authority figures who restore order,
an order that society finds necessarily contingent,
incidentally, upon possible disorder.
Those whose minds see fit to influence chaos.
These minds in disarray, order deems corrupt.
The fallacy in order is that those who it lost,
embrace the cognizance that discord must breed.
They will forevermore assure dissidence and endorse
a disharmony that the agents against chaos need
to justify their power, their force.
-Unknown

July 17th, 2012. The proceeding happened.

Jonny is an alcoholic. There is something rooted in him that inspires abhorrent behavior when he drinks, and like most alcoholics he could really fucking drink. His inebriated disposition was not easily understandable. It wasn't simply anger or an unresolved issue from his childhood or some other psychological misunderstanding or maybe it was, who knows. However he did possess a predilection towards being easily irritated when he was sober. He was easily annoyed, bothered, and fairly quick to take offense. The world was there to appease him and that is how it was and had to be. One could surmise that alcohol just heightened his anti-social sensibilities. Considering who he was sober, I think he was merely born a violent, unyielding, irrational and selfish drunk. If you were lucky enough to be one of the people Jonny tolerated on this drowning ball of chaos, you got used to it.

    I spend a lot of time with Jonny so I understand him better than most. I've been witness to his sober candor. And he is rarely sober. He seemed to always be taking out a flask or have an alcoholic beverage of some sort in his hand. Jonny wasn't oblivious to himself and how he affected the people around him. He understood that what I just described to you was who he was most of the time. He would tell you that he wasn't an ornery and obstinate person absolutely. He would say admittedly "I'm just a drunk" and shrug his shoulders. There's something ignoble about that.

    Yesterday was the Downtown Los Angeles Art Walk. It occurs on the second Thursday of every month. It was the perfect excuse to get wasted a day before the workweek ended. And that's exactly what Jonny would do on these nights. That's what I wanted to do too, that's what we all wanted to do. All being everyone in Southern California.

    You know I love to drink as well Babe, but I am a sensible drunk, a sophisticated drunk a connoisseur of wine and beer especially. Which induces me to talk because I just love to talk, as you know. Jonny wasn't that, he could become as stubborn as the telephone pole that impedes the drunk driver's car in uncontrollable and tragic peril. He becomes possessed with the same brutal force and sorrow of the crashes self-inflicted injury. Jonny is Dale Earnhardt Junior drinking a fifth of Johnnie Walker Green before the Daytona 500 then purposely plowing into Jeff Gordon and every other driver to absolve his failures. He is...

God-fucking-damnit Wolfie! What the fuck is up with this entire preface shit? Get to when I fucked that guy up on the bus, already!
Calm the fuck down you non-poetic motherfucker! I'm getting there...
And why the fuck are you speaking like I'm not in the fucking room?
I am on the phone dick head. This guy is a spy Nery. Spying on our conversation and shit.
Oh! Ahaha and you're talking about me, bitch! My ears are on fire. Hi Nery!

Any fucking way Bella, we met Jonny on 3rd & Spring Street. Mike and I walked up to Jonny who was wearing his UCLA fitted baseball cap with the bill pointed towards the moon, cutoff Levi 511 jeans because he refused to pay full price for half a pair of pants, and an Exploited "Punk's Not Dead" t-shirt. He wore a black and green flannel over the band tee with his sleeves rolled halfway up. This allowed people to know at least one thing about Jonny; that he was from Seattle. His right forearm has the Space Needle in the foreground of a gloomy Downtown Seattle skyline. He was also wearing a pair of 16 Hole Doc Martens. In his right hand was a Korean and Mexican food fusion burrito and in his left hand a cup of salsa verde. The burrito was from Calbi or one of those other Korean/Mexican fusion food trucks.

I remember this one conversation Jonny and I had in which he professed his unbridled and unadulterated hate for fusion burritos. I think this is a direct quote "I want some real Mexican shit."

Fuck that fusion shit! I wanted a real fucking burrito but there weren't any real damn Mexican food trucks represented. Ain't that some shit? The first food truck ever wasn't even allowed in the lot.

Goddammit Jonny! I'm telling the story. Quit interrupting me. And plus there are like 500 Mexican joints downtown, dumb ass.

Well, at that point in the night Jonny hadn't had a drink. Neither of us had. Like I said it was the second Thursday of the month and this was the first DTLA Artwalk of the summer. Summer Artwalks are infamous for drawing crowds into the tens of thousands. All ascending onto Gallery Row each month to indulge their cravings for creative expression whether it be a painting, a photograph, a drum circle or some weird fusion hamburger, hotdog chocolate pupusa.

I don't think we've been to the artwalk during the summer together. We'll go to the next one in August, sans Jonny, Hermosa. It's an incredible event.
Fuck you.

Every gallery on Spring Street, all the galleries on Main Street and every street in between from 2nd down to 11th were open showcasing the art of DTLA residents and their guests from all over the world. The diversity of art is amazing.

What the fuck is up with all this background shit? Get to the good shit. She doesn't give a fuck about that shit.
Esther, please control your goddamned boyfriend!
Don't be telling my bitch what to do.
Pinche puto! I'm not a bitch, bitch. I'll fuck you up Jonathan. You know I will.

You weren't talking that shit the other night. Were you Babe? Pendejo ahaha...

You know Jonny's girlfriend, Esther. She may be more insane than he is or just as insane, I don't know. Fuck it they're both fucking crazy Babe.
Shit, if she ends up dead who's crazier?
Shieeet we'll see, puto. Mirar lo que comes.

All night she and Jonny were arguing like the Montagues and Capulets. Except the jilted lovers Romeo and Juliet would be having the epic, mad, and forlorn sword fight in Verona's town square. But when Esther corners a swordless Jonny she suddenly drops her weapon and they basically fuck on the bloodstained cobble stoned streets.
That was a good one Wolfie. Me gusta. Ahaha
Corny ass nigger.

Thanks Esther. That night Esther brought along a liter of Jack Daniels, which you think would be more than enough alcohol for four people for one night. Luckily or not so luckily she did buy the liter. Jonny originally told her to buy the fifth of Jack but Esther just grabbed the first bottle she saw.
Yeah, she never listens to me.
You had fun though puto.
I did babe. Aww you know me so well Bella. You knew I'd need much more. Te amo.

Well, after Jonny finished devouring the burrito that was his hypocrisy; Jonny, Ester, Mike, and I walked towards 4th and Spring. While walking down we notice a dimly lit and very conspicuous courtyard. The building along with the courtyard belonged to the lovely people of the Federal Government, named aptly after California's greatest Governor, Ronald Reagan. The Ronald Reagan Federal building was about 30 stories tall I think. Its shadow was cast over the courtyard that was laden with tables, benches, and ashtrays for use by the FBI, Government employees and other Federal Agents during the day, transients and people seeking cover to alter their reality, as we were, at night.

The courtyard was a haven for our late night drinking. There weren't any lamps or lights and the half moon couldn't penetrate the branches of the trees that kept the courtyard separate from the Park and Save to the right of the property. The only light source that permeated our drinker's paradise was the light from the posts that lined Spring Street, about 25 feet from the area of the courtyard that Jonny, Esther, Mike and I surveyed.

After checking the area for any Federal employees, security guards, police officers and other authority figures that would frown upon our drinking, we finally opened the liter of Jack Daniels.

"I've been waiting for this all fucking day." Jonny opened the bottle then took a swig. He then popped open a Mexican Coke using the bottle opener he kept on his keys, took a huge gulp and passed both bottles to me. I did the same then passed the bottles to Esther. We took swig after swig, drink after drink and gulp after gulp until the bottle was a little more than half full. Everyone but Mike partook of the bottle. Mike isn't a fan of Jack Daniels, he's a vodka man...

You did give his gay ass some cinnamon tasting shit. What was it? Fireball? He drank the shit out of that pussy shit.
Shut the fuck up Jonny! He got drunk like we all did.
No he didn't. He didn't get drunk like me.
I bet he's glad he didn't too.
I am. Because I would have fucked you... Joto.

Jonny and I sat on one bench and directly across from us were Esther and Mike...

You remember when I called their bench the woman's section? That was a good one.
What a homophobic clown Jonny is. I am sorry Bella.

If you like getting fucked, you're a woman. Just kidding man I'm only fucking around. You know I'm kidding right Mike? I love fags. I love you too Esther, baby.
I know you do Jonny, you fucking ass hole.
Ay Babe.
Half the liter of Jack was gone, Mike had drunk most of the Fireball, which was about half full when I gave it to him, Jonny put the bottles into his bag and we finally decided that we were tipsy enough to get our night started. We needed to be a tad inebriated to fit in with the pretentious folks who supposed that Michelangelo's David meant something greater and insightful than "Michelangelo was a homo." It was time to explore some galleries.

    We gathered ourselves at the entrance to the courtyard then we made a left beginning our southern trek down Spring Street. We noticed that the first few art galleries, which were about 100 feet from where we were previously, were all closed. We passed the Bang Gallery, Robert Reynolds's Gallery, and Miguel Osuna's Art Studio all of which usually had people spilling into the streets trying to get in. They had been seemingly abandoned. It was about 9:15PM and on Art Walk Thursdays most galleries wouldn't close until Midnight some even later. But still, tipsy and hardly inquisitive we continued on our journey to intake DTLA's celebration of human expression.

    On Art Walk nights Jonny would usually call me from a bar to see if I wanted to embrace the spectacle. Not so much the art but the crowded bar scene. We seldom walked from gallery to gallery or enjoyed the street performances or exhibitions. Frankly, we never absorbed any art. We would get plastered and then I'd sit back and watch Jonny get into arguments over billiards. I think it was because he had worked every art walk for about two years and had exhausted his admiration for the event. But this day was different.

The art fucking sucks now. Well some of it is still amazing I guess, on some shitty shit. I remember before all the hype and all the food trucks every gallery had killer exhibits because you fucking had to have some great shit to get people to come to Gallery Row. It smells like piss everywhere down there. No one wants to smell piss and see some shitty shit.

Stop with the fucking soliloquys already. Please let me get through this you motherfucker, so we can get out of here. *Sorry. You're acting like a bitch right now though.*

This time it was the group's collective goal to ensure that Mike had a memorable night. This was Mike's first artwalk and Jonny was actually excited to make sure he had a great time. He also hadn't stepped foot into any of the galleries or enjoyed any of the street performances in awhile. He wanted to see what the artists in the neighborhood new and old had been working on.

The Jack Daniels was beginning to take a greater effect. Esther, who is very capricious sober, had gotten mad at Jonny because she believed he was looking at some mildly attractive woman walking her dog. They were too busy arguing and Mike and I were too busy listening that we failed to notice that there weren't any cars traveling down Spring Street. Usually around 9:30PM on these nights there was bumper-to bumper-traffic. I look back towards 4th Street and Parking Enforcement was disallowing vehicles to travel south. Traffic was being diverted down 4th.

When I looked towards Jonny and Esther, who were about 15 feet in front of Mike and I, they had stopped arguing and walking. We were now in the middle of Spring Street between 4th and 5th where the city is developing an old parking lot into a park. We catch up to the tumultuous lovers who had stopped in awe of the hundreds of people in the middle of what should have been a traffic-ridden street. We walked with timid astonishment slowly passing promoters handing out flyers, drunken yuppies, hipsters, homeless people, couples with dogs and artists selling their canvases inflicted with stencils of Bob Marley, Marilyn Monroe, and Tupac. The crowd was enamored with something or some event. As we passed the unfinished park, Bolt Barbershop and Buzz Beer and Wine we ascended upon the crowd's adoration.

 This was the first Art Walk of the summer, also the most crowded, and unbeknownst to anyone who was not apart of Occupy Los Angeles, the Occupy camp were planning a huge protest against the establishment, I guess. The huge crowd in attendance was perfect for disseminating a simple message quickly. A message I'm ignorant of but I guess is capitalism, big banks, the police, and anyone who does not adhere to their program, whatever that is, are responsible for why they can't find work. Something along those lines.

 I'm protesting against Occupy LA for lack of hygiene. Them motherfuckers stink! One tried to talk to me the other day about some Capitalism shit. I damn near passed out. I seen about three or four other motherfuckers already knocked out on the sidewalk below this motherfucker. People hopping over them and shit. They need to pass out those SARS masks before they start speaking to people.

 Okay Jonny. In between a wall of riot gear clad police officers in the middle of 5th street on the eastside of Spring and a wall of LAPD officers in the middle of Spring street on the southside of 5th, was the true cause of all the commotion, chalk drawings.

 The intersection at 5th and Spring looked like an anarchist elementary school playground. "Down with Capitalism" "Hang the bankers" "We are the 99%" the always apt and essentially quintessential "Fuck the police" and other extrapolations of Occupy rhetoric littered the intersection. The Down N Out on the southwest corner of the intersection, Orcas on the southeast, Buzz and Bolt on the northeast, and the Crocker Club on the northwest, were all shut down. The LAPD wouldn't allow anyone to enter or exit until almost 4 in the morning.

It would have been fucking awesome to be trapped in the DnO or Orcas or The Crocker Club. I've been getting texts all morning about all the free shots the owners of businesses on Gallery Row were handing out. That would have been fucking awesome.

We didn't stay on Spring for long. The Occupy protesters began throwing bottles and rocks and chanting the same slogans that were temporarily tattooed on the pavement...

Why the fuck were those pork chop sandwich, pastry gorging motherfuckers mad that they were drawing on the concrete with chalk? What the fuck is that shit? What the fuck is next? What, a littering ticket for plucking rose pedals? She loves me. She loves me fucking not. I bet if I dumped out a bottle of Evian water onto the street they'd cite me for toxic waste dumping.

Shut the fuck up Jonny. Esther control your boyfriend, please!

I can control him just as well as you can Wolfie. The fucker is loco. ¿Tú quieres mi pinocha anoche? ¡Cállate pues! I'll shut the fuck up. I'll shut up. Only if you promise some head too.

¡Ay pinche puto, Jonathan!

For fuck sakes, Babe. Well, we were there for about an half hour observing and anticipating the LAPD's response to the occupier's bottle throwing which was highly inaccurate. Then suddenly without any warning at all. No stop or we'll shoot, we're going to rush you motherfuckers and start whooping ass, nothing of the sort. The cops directly across from the crowd of Art Walk patrons began to rush forward.

Without any hesitation the crowd scattered towards 4th street. Officers were screaming "get the fuck back" "clear the street" with a fury that was obviously misplaced rage dedicated to the "Occupiers." The crowd of hipsters, spoiled Black kids, the rich Latinos, and Asian tourists ran for their lives.

Rich Latinos? This motherfucker right here! You know damn well they were selling bacon wrapped hot dogs. And spoiled Blacks? What about that broke ass nigger who asked you for 50 cents? Them Asians just kept taking pictures. They didn't give a fuck...
Ay! ¿No tú quieres que yo a chupar tu pene bitch?
Si Bella, lo siento. I'm sorry babe.
Now you owe me head stupid ass.
¿Sesenta y nueve?
¡Ay Panson!
¡Vámonos Wolfie, shit!

If you would shut the fuck up I could be done already, damn! Ok Hermosa. So this crowd of people from all different backgrounds and cultures began to run back towards 4th street and we followed. The action proved just to be a threat and they didn't further intimidate the crowd. The southside officers then reverted back to their original position. Jonny was running like a bitch.

Soon after the feigned threat the LAPD sent warnings through a megaphone, "Please disperse or you will be subject to arrest," "clear the area," and such. Shots from rubber bullets, sirens, megaphone declarations and tear gas influenced screams would frame our night. But we would get too fucking wasted and wrapped up in Jonny's dysfunction to realize what was happening around us. I didn't find out about all the ass whooping's and arrests until this morning. I saw that shit on fucking KCAL. And we were right fucking there!

We got the fuck out of there. I guess that spurious threat by the LAPD kept us away from last night's chaotic discord. We just assumed that the street would be shut down and that the crowd would eventually disperse. We never figured that a riot would ensue and officers and citizens would fight the first battle of the revolution on those streets. Besides we wanted to continue getting hammered.

We decided to not attempt to see if the galleries south of the fracas were open and headed back to Reagan's courtyard. Jonny had a wonderful idea, asinine in hindsight, "Let's go grab a six pack." No one dissented. We made a right on 4th, walked down to Main Street then took a right passed the Old Bank Merchants Banquet Hall, Salon on Main, and into the Old Bank Market.

Jonny walked straight to the beer aisle and grabbed a six-pack of Negra Modelo. Esther grabbed a bag of Jalapeno Kettle Chips, Mike grabbed a can of Coke and I grabbed a bottle of water. I knew hydration was going to be needed because we just drank half of a liter of Jack Daniels, still had a half a liter to go and we just bought a six-pack. Jonny, being the nice guy that he is paid for all of our items and then we were on our way back to the Federal Building.

Instead of walking back down 4th Street to Spring and then making a right to get to the courtyard, we walked north up Main to 3rd to show Mike more of the Art Walk. There aren't any galleries in-between 4th and 3rd so Mike still hasn't seen any art. The spectacle of drunk art elitists, bucket drum drummers banging for change, and girls playing Double Dutch on the sidewalk was plenty entertaining and more or less artful itself. As I always tell you, bearing a bit of pretention, art is just expression.
Corny ass nigga!

While Mike and I were admiring the eclecticism of culture that was the crowd, Jonny had already opened one of the bottles of Negra Modelo. Enjoying it out in the open like he was on Las Vegas Boulevard or like it was Mike's Coca

Cola. "This isn't Mardi Gras Jonny. Put that shit away. Don't you see cops all around us?"

"Of course I see them but fuck all that. They're not worried about us. I'm just having fun, bro. I'm not doing shit. They're more worried about those Occupy clowns."

Jonny was right. The morning after I read on the Los Angeles Times website that dozens of calls to dispatchers of the 100 N Main Police Station and the station in Skid Row on 6th and Central were to disregard emergency calls because of the grand presence that was necessitated by the standoff on 5th and Spring. There were 600 overtime hours and over 200 officers called to quell the uproarious chalking by the occupiers, and not one would stop Jonny from drinking his beer. I don't think he knew that at the time, although he seemingly professed so. I know he was wasted, so he probably didn't give a fuck or at least was willing to accept the consequences.

Mike and I were walking ahead of Jonny and Esther attempting to enjoy the night. "Are you having fun Mike?" I inquired because to this point we hadn't seen a painting, sculpture, or even heard any music that was organized or neatly presented. "Yeah it's been pretty fun. Seeing all these pretty people is all I need an it's better than being in the fucking house all night," Mike answered candidly.

"I mean; are you disappointed that we haven't seen any art? This is your first art walk, you know."

"I'm just having fun with you guys."

As Mike and I approached 3rd and Main Street Mike noted, "Where are Esther and Jonny? They've been pretty quiet." We hadn't heard anything from them in a few minutes, which was immediately dumbfounding. We looked back to see what was keeping the demented sweethearts and Jonny was in the Double Dutch line waiting his turn. Esther was standing to the side of him with a huge grin on her face.

Mike and I walked back and joined Esther's side. "Girl, your smile is amazing by the way. But why are you smiling so sinisterly," Mike wondered. "Jonathan's going to fuck up. Watch," Esther responded with constrained delight.

  They're a volatile couple that seems to dislike each other very much or more than most couples. They hate each other with an uncanny vigor. If you dropped them together on Hiroshima on Nagasaki there would be no such thing as Sony or Toyota. If they flew into the Twin Towers, New York City would be in the middle of the Atlantic. They could swallow a black hole or commit an atheist to Christ and the opposite. There individual spite had to be reckoned with but together going at each other's throats it was like combining Two Hydrogen atoms with two Oxygen atoms. They were each other's worst enemy. They knew each other too well and loved to exploit what they knew.

  What Esther knew is why she was smiling so devilishly. She knew that Jonny couldn't Double Dutch and also knew that she couldn't convince him otherwise. She found his determination vacuous but cute.

  It was Jonny's turn to jump-in and with a sizeable crowd of spectators cheering him on similarly to all the previous participants, giving him the added confidence that the alcohol already in his blood didn't.

  One turn, two turns, three turns. Jonny then jumped in like a pro. The two jump ropes passed successfully under his feet for the first six hops but on the seventh his feet got tangled in the ropes. In an attempt to keep himself from falling he grabbed both of the jump ropes, snatching them from one of the turners and pulling the other with him to the ground. The horrific moment when this woman figured that her hitting the pavement was inevitable was incensed on her face. As she hit the ground 10 feet from the back entrance to the Ronald Reagan Building, "What the fuck is wrong with you, you drunk asshole!?" She hit the concrete a second or two after Jonny. Esther now unconstrained, erupted in unconcerned for her boyfriend's well being, no concern for the poor woman who was dragged to the ground by her boyfriend's affected coordination, laughter.

She knew what Jonny would have known sober but couldn't know drunk that he couldn't Double Dutch. He could barely walk drunk. He's not a clumsy individual but when he was drunk he was a wrecking ball.

"I did pretty good huh, babe? I was killing it!" Jonny said with complete disregard of the woman whose night he had just ruined. It did not faze Jonny. All the cheers that transformed into laughter he deflected. It was as if he was deaf or something. None of the jeering affected his disposition or mannerisms. Shoulders straight and head high he grabbed the Negra Modelo that a laugh possessed Esther was holding for him, he took a swig and we continued on our way.

"Look at this bitch. Ahaha" Jonny notices a drunken girl walking in heels stumbling in the middle of the crosswalk on 3rd and Spring. She manages to stumble through the crosswalk only to fall on the corner where our night began. "Glad I'm not that drunk," Jonny remarked. She jumps back on her feet as quickly as she fell and laughs awkwardly. It was as if the faster she stood up the quicker she could hear the laughs and ridicule and the quicker we'd all forget about it. She'd laugh to help absolve some of it as well. She collects herself; her embarrassment seemingly eased then Jonny screams to her, "Can't hang huh? She's done for the night!" Esther quickly grabs his arm and next thing you know we were back in Reagan's courtyard.

Helicopter rotors and sirens displaced the voices of the Art Walk patrons who headed ignorantly into the standoff that ended our art seeking. It was weird that none of them thought anything of the sirens or gunshots. Well, neither did we. Mike remarked, "Were those gunshots?"

"No they weren't motherfucker. Let's drink," Jonny responded as he took a swig of Jack Daniels.

The Los Angeles Times website also reported that the LAPD had fired over 100 rubber bullets and beanbags into the crowd of Occupiers. 31 Occupiers were injured, 20 of those were arrested. Most of the injuries were concussions and internal bleeding. Must have been a lot of headshots.

Jonny already had two of the Negra Modelos and was drinking from the liter of Jack. I take two and Esther takes the remaining two. Mike continued to drink the Fireball. Mike and Esther were enriching their lives talking about some Lady Gaga song they both liked. Jonny and I were talking about random shit, smoking a bowl of LA Confidential. As I am putting the pipe to my lips our dimly lit haven is illuminated by a detective's vehicle that drives onto the sidewalk directly in front of the benches were we sat. It drives down Spring on the sidewalk still full with people, he sped unabated towards the battleground. Jonny and I run out of the courtyard to see what was going on, and all we could see were blue and red lights reflecting off of the droves of people scurrying in terror.

A little impatient and over-zealous if you ask me. I guess mowing down hundreds of innocent people is worth keeping Occupy LA from playing hopscotch in the middle of the fucking street.

After I finished my two beers I join Esther and Jonny in finishing the liter of Jack. Esther, Mike nor I thought for one second to keep Jonny from himself and tell him to chill out. The bottle of Jack was not being distributed equally, Jonny had probably drunk 2/3rds of it on his own, drinking way more than his fair share.

We were all pretty fucked up, getting louder, more rowdy and more animated when we spoke to each other. But Jonny's disposition became incredibly more unsettled. Sober, as I said before, he's a confrontational person and seems to easily misconstrue simple situations into attacks upon his person, warranted or unwarranted. But drunk I mean wasted out of his fucking mind? He was a nuclear weapon and some unlucky fucker was bound to become the detonator. That unlucky bastard would be incinerated.

One thing that makes me like him and put up with his insecure self-destruction is that he is always fun to talk to. Jonny is mildly educated. He knows what he believes and is more open minded than most. For instance, Jonny and I were discussing gender equality last night for some reason:

"If a woman hits me, I'm hitting her back I don't give a fuck!"

"But what about your strength advantage? What if it was your sister or your mother? Don't you believe that women are physically a bit more fragile than a man?"

"Some of them. My sister and my mother should know better not to hit someone unless they want to be hit. Do women who hit men in the back of their mind's figure that he isn't going to hit them back because it isn't a popular societal convention? Fuck that shit! My mom always told me that if a woman or anyone hits you, you knock that motherfucker out!"

"But it isn't a fair fight. Look at how big you are. Boxing and MMA have weight classes for a reason. You mean if Esther hits you you're going to hit her back? This isn't eye for an eye that's like eye for both of her legs. Your size alone makes her hits futile."

"Esther and I have been in plenty of fist fights. She can handle her shit."

Esther interrupts, "You're fucking right I can, Bitch"

Jonny continued, "Yes you can Bella. But it's the principal. Don't think you can hit someone and them not fuck you up. That's crazy psychology. The woman's initial violence that was going to cause some sort of reaction is completely denied because the man she hit gave her a two piece special and a biscuit and she is now knocked out in between the couch and the end table, snoring. Her action is negated? I don't think you should knock your woman out but if you hit her back you both should be punished or it should be labeled self-defense. That's gender equality. Don't hit me with the expectation not to be hit. Any woman who says that it's okay for a woman to hit a man and that it's wrong for a man to hit a woman deserves every tenant of the patriarchy."

You see a very interesting, backwards, morbid and eerily valid point of view. I guess that's his way of saying no one should hit anyone unless it is in self-defense. So I guess no one would ever hit anyone. Jonny has framed the perfect world!

We sat in the courtyard for a good hour talking about politics and sex. "Fuck voting and I love fucking," seemed to be Jonny's sentiments.

"What about Measure B? Or Prop 30? Those both affect you," Mike asks.

"Just not my thing. Too much shit points to us being powerless. Cities and states are still going to abuse their budget and these snake politicians are trained to find loopholes."

"You need to vote babe," interjects Esther. "At least for Measure B. Condoms in porn is unnatural and shitty."

"That is true. But there are so many condomless pornos I haven't seen. I can jerk off to those, ahaha. Or you can help me baby."

"Pendejo"

"I wonder what the far right thinks about Measure B?"

"Those bitches are probably for it."

Esther had been drinking the Jack Daniels and chasing it with Negra Modelo. She was visibly wasted and passed the rest of her second beer to Jonny. Jonny took both the beer and liter from his drunken girlfriend. He emptied the rest of the liter of Jack then chugged the Negra Modelo. "Let's go get another six-pack," he urged. I was more than willing to drink some more and so was Mike, Esther was the only one to disagree because she knew her limit and was done drinking for the night.

We left the courtyard and walked back down 4th Street to Main and back to the Old Bank Market that was now closed.

"What the fuck? It's only 11:30."

Pete's, Baco Mercat, and the newly opened Kitchen Table across the street were all closed as well. All of which were usually open until 2AM. Since every restaurant, shop, and bar, all the places that sold or served alcohol were closed, we decided to take the train back to my place, stop by the liquor store on the corner of Olympic and Normandie, and pick up a 12 pack of beer. I was certain that Olympic Liquor had not been affected by the upheaval on Gallery Row.

We turnaround and headed west on 4th Street passed Spring, passed Broadway to the 4th and Hill subway station. We hopped on the escalator down to the station's entrance and it was closed. A huge gate impeded any movement into or out of the station. It's about 11:45PM now and the Red Line typically runs until 1AM on weekdays. The MTA apparently was ordered, just as the other businesses in the area, to shut down the Pershing Square Station because of the disorder on 5th and Spring, Gallery Row was only two blocks away from the station.

Jonny wasn't too happy about that; "What the fuck is going on here? Everything is fucking closed goddamnit! Let me in this motherfucker!" He shook the steel gate like he was unlawfully imprisoned and screamed at the top of his lungs "open this goddamn gate" as if that was exactly how the MTA opened the station every morning. Jonny then became very quiet for the first time all night. His face was flustered; he stared blankly at the steel, he shook his head in disgust. This was Jonny at stasis, his emotions being suffocated by a pillow of frustration. He was like a dormant volcano before lava and ash buried the nearest town or the eye of a hurricane or a nice day at the beach before a tsunami disfigures your peace and paradise.

Jonny erupted. I imagine that he thought that his punches would tear the gate down like the Berlin Wall but the gate almost broke his knuckles it left them gashed and bloody. As he punched he didn't say a word, he didn't scream or order the gate to open. He just punched and punched with all of his strength. If the gate could feel, it would be begging for mercy. But as the gate couldn't feel seemingly Jonny couldn't either or at least he didn't show it. He didn't recognize that he had just maimed his hands and for a reason that was out of his control.

Esther finally grabbed Jonny and we walked back up the escalator that was now just a set of stairs. Since the train wasn't an option we decided to catch the 720 bus on 5th and Broadway. It would then drop us off on Wilshire and Western. We could buy a 12 pack at Ralph's then walk down Oxford to San Marino, then San Marino to Ardmore to my apartment.

When we reached street level Jonny forgets about the train because he sees a huge John Jameson Irish Whiskey advertisement at the bus stop on the corner of 4th and Hill Street. "That poster would be so fucking sick on any fucking wall in my apartment." Then Jonny without hesitation charged shoulder first at the partition that was housing the object of his deranged affection. This forced the homeless man on the bus stop's bench out of his sleep and startled the three teenaged girls and what looked to be their boyfriends waiting for the number 4 bus. Jonny must have believed, as he did with the train station gate, that he could destroy the barrier between what he wanted and what he had to accept with determined vigorous violence. The partition proved stronger than Jonny's bum rush and was unfazed.

"Just like the gate, huh Babe?" Esther instigates. Jonny didn't look back at her; he was quiet then began to kick the shit out of the thick plastic window that covered the poster. He couldn't get what he wanted but he could make a shit load of noise.

People in line at La Cita across the street and patrons of Jose's Tacos stared. Mike and I stood there in awe of his disregard for everyone and everything around him but also admired his determination. Jonny walked back a couple of feet then charged the partition once again but this time with a Liu Kang from Mortal Combat jump kick. The jump kick was ineffective and Jonny fell on his back and did a backwards barrel roll away from the bottle of Jameson and landed at the feet of his girlfriend. Esther stood their laughing at Jonny's futility as she had been doing all night. Jonny then rose to his feet and stomped angrily down Hill Street. Like a child who wanted Captain Crunch but instead his mother bought Raisin Bran.

On the southwest corner of 5th and Hill, south across the street from the number 4 bus stop is an apartment building. Jonny stopped at the secure front entrance of this apartment building and noticed a potted tree to the right of the front door and directly in front of a window that is in front of the security guard's desk.

Inexplicably, with disregard for the security guard, Jonny begins many unavailing attempts to uproot the tree from its potted prison. Using the same incessant and staunch effort as the barrage of punches on the gate and the many kicks to the bus stop partition. Mike and I were simply confused while Esther continued to antagonize Jonny's efforts, "You can't do it. Fuck it! Just give up."

"Fuck that shit, Esther! As soon as I get this tree out I'm fucking you up with it! I'm going to beat the shit out of you with this fucking tree! You better not run or leave," Jonny shouted short of breath.

"Yeah right puto!" replied Esther chuckling. Jonny, loud and disorderly his mangled bloody hands strangling this poor tree was then approached by a man on a bicycle. The guy takes off his helmet and says to Jonny while dismounting "What are you doing dude? I live in this building." Jonny drops the tree and replies "I don't give a fuck where you live motherfucker! Fuck you!" And continues to strangle the tree.

I don't know why this guy felt it was his duty to approach a 6'3" 220 pound angry man with blood all over his hands trying to pull a tree out of a pot, but he did.

"What's your problem man? I live here. Get the fuck out of here."

"Fuck you, you punk bitch. Go up to your fucking apartment and mind your own fucking business," Jonny said stepping towards the bicyclist completely forgetting about the tree. The two were now face to face and Jonny towered over this man who had to be about 5'8" or 5'9" and maybe 150 to 160 pounds. Jonny hunched over, their noses a sneeze away from touching, "You better calm the fuck down before I flatten you, you fucking pussy," he promised.

"Fuck you, asshole!" The biker then pushed Jonny and in the milliseconds before Jonny could react he was grabbed by two of the apartment's security guards and Mike. There was unbridled fury in his eyes.

This wasn't an inanimate gate, bus stop partition, or baby tree. He locked onto the bicyclist's eyes and if Jonny were able to do what he wanted to do to him that guy would have been forcibly transformed into a different person. Like he would have a different face because Jonny would have ripped him apart. This very lucky bicyclist would have surely regretted further enraging a big man with bloody hands who was attempting to hit his girlfriend with a tree.

While the two apartment security guards and Mike were keeping Jonny from killing that lucky bastard, I attempted to keep Esther from murdering the same dumb motherfucker.

"Who the fuck are you pushing bitch?! Don't ever touch my man!" Before I could get Esther away she slapped the fucking shit out of the bicyclist. She slapped him so hard that he did a 360 degrees spin and almost knocked over his bike. Which wobbled but was saved from the pavement by its kickstand.

A third security guard grabbed Esther and now both members of the fervid couple were being restrained by the apartment building's security. This motherfucker, this facial reconstruction-avoiding bastard then turned to me and said, "Control your fucking friends man. I'm just protecting my home."

I responded, "That's why you fucking have security asshole. You're lucky you have security too. They saved your ass from being demolished."

The situation dissolved as soon as the cyclist grabbed his bike and walked into the building. The security guards let Jonny and Esther go and when they were assured that we all were a safe distance away they soon followed the cyclist into the building.

"I bet that exciting episode will keep them awake for about 15 minutes," Mike snickered.

And then in another moment of impossible explication Jonny started running down Hill Street, jumping up and pulling down branches and leaves from each tree in his path. It wasn't just incredible that he was doing this it was awesome that he was jumping so high in Doc Martins.

"Esther?"

"¿Que pasò Wolfie?"

"What the fuck is wrong with your boyfriend? Jesus fucking Christ."

"No sé. El es un borracho."

"He's not drunk all the time though," interjects Mike.

"He can't be like this all of the time."

"No es. Esta noche está loco."

"You think? ¡Esto es el caos!" I tell her.

"Es gracioso."

About 100 feet ahead of us Jonny is still running and pulling down branches when he stops abruptly staring upward. We wade through the fallen twigs, branches and leaves and when we get to within 20 feet of Jonny he jumps up with both arms extended and tries to pull down a branch that had to be at least ten feet high in the air. His blood covered hands fail to get a full grip, he slips off, falls forward and lands right on his face. Mike, Esther, and I with nervous concern run to his side to see if he's okay. He hops up as soon as we get to within five feet, stumbling. I didn't know if it was from landing on his head or just drunken mechanics.

"Are you okay Jonny. Jonny stop. Are you okay?"

"Babe? ¿Estás bien? ¿Estás bien Jonathan?"

"Stop Jonny. Chill out for a second. Come on Wolfie lets grab him," Mike asserts.

We all run after him and force him to stop.

"Why are we stopping? We have to get to the bus stop and then to the liquor store."

"Babe, look at your face. You need to calm down Jonathan. Pinche calmarse!"

"Yeah man. Your face is all scratched up and your nose is bleeding."

"I don't give a fuck! You think I give a fuck?" Jonny then turns to the No Parking sign 30 feet from the corner of Hill and 5th and unloads punches with double the fury of the blows he threw at the steel gate.

"I don't give a fuck! I should have thrashed that guy and his security. Let's go back. Fuck that shit! Let's find that bitch! Let's go back."

"We're not going back Jonny."

"Come on Babe. Let's go. Por favor mi amor!"

As he's punching the pole Jonny screams, "I'll knock on every door in that fucking building! Let's go back and find that motherfucker! He fucking pushed me and got away with it!"

Jonny eventually stops punching the pole and then looks at his hands, hands that looked like he lathered them with glass. He threw his head down and then walked somberly towards 5th street.

"Let's get to the liquor store Jonny," I tell him in an attempt to cheer him up, console him. He lifts his head, chuckles, and his attention is diverted back to getting more alcohol into his system. It was a nasty fall. Pretty funny in hindsight but I'm surprised he didn't sustain a concussion or break his face. He fell right on his fucking head. It was like a ghost gave him a DDT or something.

We make a left on 5th towards our absolution, our way to avoid any further turmoil that night. But 5th street east of Broadway was still being barricaded by the LAPD. Officers and their squad cars stood single file mirroring each other's inanimateness. The street was inoperable to cars and busses. The Rite Aid on the southeast corner, the 7 Eleven on the southwest, and the Fallas Paredes on the same corner as the bus stop were all closed.

"Where can we catch the 720? Where is the detour?" Jonny asked one of the officers. And like a guard outside of Buckingham Palace the officer didn't flinch.

"Where's the damn detour? Y'all ain't doing shit. Where's the motherfucking detour at?"

"Come on Jonathan. ¡Vámonos ahora!"

Mike and Esther pull Jonny up Broadway back to 4th street. We walk down Broadway towards 5th and make a right heading east back towards Main. Our intention was to catch the bus at the 5th and Main stop. In our drunkenness we failed to deduce that all of 5th street was inaccessible. Especially considering that Broadway and Main were only about three blocks away from each other. The police cars and wagons covered all four lanes of the street.

Main in between 4th and 5th had become a parking lot similar to 5th and Broadway. Surprisingly, huge crowds still roamed the street despite the fact that all of the businesses and galleries in the area were closed. Some were Occupy Los Angeles demonstrators; some were simply opportunists but all were tagging the copious proverbs of the Occupy movement onto the most intimidating cars on the road and only 20 feet from the officers that drove them, who were still under order not to react to anything but overt violence, apparently. Otherwise I'm pretty sure someone would have been beaten, especially Jonny. Jonny would have gotten his ass whooped.

Nah, they would have had to shoot me.

And I bet they would have. Jonny saw what was going on and inferred whatever it was he inferred. He then jumped onto the hood of the nearest police cruiser and proceeded to jump from police car to police car down the block like he was tearing down tree branches once again. He ran on the hood, up the windshield, onto the roof, down the rear window glass and then onto the trunk of about six Crown Victoria's. He finally jumped off and into the face of three Occupiers tagging what would have been the seventh vehicle.

"What the fuck are you clowns talking about? We are the 99 percent? Fuck that bullshit. You guys are fucking nuts. You think those in the 80 to 98.999 percent give a fuck about you guys and all this bullshit? Got all these coppers out here for no fucking reason. Fuck those cops. Fuck y'all too! Y'all 99 percent bitch!"

Jonny grabs a marker that was on the ground and writes his name in sloppy capital letters on the cruiser.

"Oh shit! Your name is on this car Wolfie? Who the fuck did that?"

"I did man. While you were chastising those guys I was going to work," I proudly replied.

"That shit looks super sick motherfucker. Esther take a picture of me with this shit."

All of this in view of the Los Angeles Police Department's finest. And still the cops didn't move one inch displaying an uncanny, soldier like discipline.

"Look at you guys. Wasting my money. Quit wasting my money. Go do some shit. Y'all ain't doing shit. Just standing there. 'Oh my! We need 100,000 officers for 10 people. We ain't shit! We ain't shit!' You clowns aren't shit! Get the fuck out of here! You're not doing a goddamn thing but ruining the Art Walk!"

"Come on Jonny. Let's go! Let's get the fuck out of here. We can catch the bus at 5th and Grand. That must be where it detours."

We grab Jonny and walk down 5th back to Broadway. In the middle of the long block in between Spring and Broadway, we see the 720 making a left turn onto 5th street and stopping at the Broadway stop. The 720's detour route was to make a left down Central, take Central to 7th Street, then make a right onto Broadway, left onto 5th Street, back on route to the City of Santa Monica. Luckily there was a wheelchair getting off of the bus or else we wouldn't have made it. It was about 1:00 am at this point.

"We're going to make it to the liquor store Jonny. I know your ass is happy."

"Yeah now we're all happy, babe."

"Fuck that shit. I would be happy if I would have flattened that fucking biker motherfucker. Turned that motherfucker into Looney Tunes. Wild E. Coyote or Porky Pig or a pancake or something. I was ready to unload on that piece of shit. I'm dying to unload on that motherfucker. Damn I would have fucked him up. Let's go back! Let's fucking go back! He's so fucking lucky he isn't in the hospital right now."

Again, I just don't understand why anyone would agitate Jonny especially if he wasn't directly or deliberately agitating them and especially if they noticed his very bloody hands, shirt, face, and pants. But from the center seat of the bus, the seat that turns as the bus turns, some guy interrupts, "Shut the fuck up dude. You wouldn't have done shit otherwise you would have. Only bitches talk shit after the fact."

"What the fuck did you say to me bitch?"

Jonny was sitting in the high aisle facing seats above the bus's right wheel well by himself. Mike and Esther were sitting directly across from him on the left side of the bus, and I was on the same side of the bus as Jonny holding onto the ceiling bars.

Jonny's most recent agitator was sitting, as I've said, in the center bus seat that turns as the bus turns. This seat is considerably lower than where Jonny sat.

"What the fuck did you say?" Jonny asked again.

And in the same breath he stepped down from his seat putting his left foot down first and in the same motion and breath kicked the guy hard in the face with his right foot. Once his feet are both planted he throws a right upper cut and a left jab that make this fool's head snap back like a Pez dispenser. The bus driver stops the bus and before Jonny can put the finishing touches on this imbecilic guy the bus driver yells, "Hey! What the Hell is going on back there? Get off the bus or I'm calling the police."

"Come on get off the bus so I can fuck you up."

"Correrle Jonathan. What the fuck are you doing? El esta llamando la policia! Con prisa!" Esther urges.

"Let's go Jonny. You don't want to go to jail," warns Mike.

"I don't give a fuck. Fuck this dude. Should have minded his fucking business. While throwing two last shots at his head."

Jonny exits the bus. Pounding on the window to get his latest antithesis to follow but the guy didn't see him. He just sat in his seat, head in his lap. His two friends, who sat there in shock while their friend was getting his ass beat, consoled him.

"I'm out of here. Fuck that shit. I'm tired of you guys not letting me do what the fuck I want to do. See you motherfuckers later." Jonny then walks away.

"Jonathan espera! Espera Jonathan! I'm sorry you guys. I'm so so sorry. I'll have him call you tomorrow Wolfie." Esther then runs after Jonny.

"Damn that motherfucker's crazy Wolfie. I have never experienced anything like this before in my life."

"That's Jonny. He gets wasted and doesn't give a shit. Did you at least have fun?"

"Yeah it was fun. It wasn't funny all the time but Jonny falling on his face was fucking priceless. Damn…"
"Ahaha I know man. I'm surprised he got up from that."
"He might have a concussion, I'm serious. I hope Esther doesn't let him go to sleep. Ahaha"
Since Jonny got us all kicked off of the bus Mike and I had to walk the six miles or so back to my apartment. But before we got home we stopped at the Denny's on Wilshire and Oxford and had a cup of coffee. We couldn't stop laughing at that guy's head being snapped back like he was Soda Pop from Mike Tyson's Punch Out.
Jonny didn't call me this morning but he apologized for last night in person. That's why he and Esther are here right now. Well babe that's what happened last night. That's why I forgot to call you and that's why I got home so late. It was Jonny's fault.

Bye Nery! Finally motherfucker. I thought I told you to hurry the fuck up and tell the fucking story? Let's get out of here. We're late for happy hour.
Hold the fuck on… Nery wanted to know what happened last night. I'll see you in a bit Babe. Remember we're meeting at The Gold Room. See you in a minute, bye baby.
Final-fucking-ly Wolfie. You're too long winded man.
Shut up Jonathan, damn. It was a great story Wolfie. Me encanto.
I did fuck that guy up on the bus though and I would have fucked up the other dude too. That was a nice slap babe. I didn't even know you did that. That's why I love you!
Ay Jonathan, Te amo también pero correrle Wolfie. I'm thirsty.
Okay let's go. They serve the tequila and a pint special all night Jonny so don't fucking worry.

Well let's just fucking go I'm tired of sitting here. First round on Wolfie! Fuck, last night was so hardcore.
Fue caos.

Trust Your Lover's Phone

A cat scurried underneath Jonny's feet followed by three of its kittens. Two other cats lay at the base of the lemon tree; three others and many more kittens were stacked on top of each other fighting for their mother's milk. One more cat lay on the back porch of the lots main house. Esther lived in the lot's duplex with her mother, stepfather, and two siblings. Dogs barked as many more kittens scurried between his slow moving feet. The sun had risen but cocks still crowed as if they were shouting down the sun.

"Flaca! Flaca! Hurry the fuck up, I thought that you were ready?" Jonny yelled.

"I am fucking ready. Don't be yelling like that in my house."

"You said you were ready, you always have me waiting all fucking day for you."

"Just shut the fuck up Jonathan and let's go."

Esther descended the stairs and her and Jonny walked from under the lemon and tangerine trees that brushed Jonny's face, like he brushed off spider webs.

Esther closed the lots main gate, "I think you should tie your shoes babe." The lovers were walking to the liquor store to buy some beer. While he typed on his phone, "I'll do it in a second," Jonny responded.

"Ahora, mi amor. You might trip and fall," Esther urged.

"Bella, I have never tripped and fell because of my goddamn shoe laces being untied. That's a myth," Jonny continued to type.

"Why must you always argue with me Jonathan? Just tie your fucking zapatos."

"What the fuck is the big deal? Calm the fuck down! We're at the store already. Now I'll tie them," Jonny bent down and angrily tied his size thirteen black Chuck Taylors.

"Jesus fucking H-Christ, Esther. Are you happy, for fuck sakes? Now go get the fucking tall boys, please? I'll pay for them."

Jonny approached the register and pulled out a bag filled with nickels, dimes, and a few quarters to pay for the four tall cans of Miller High Life, two for him and two for Esther.

"That will be eight dollars even."

"Sorry about all of the coins Mr. Kim, it's that time of the month again, sadly."

"It's okay Jonny I needed change for the register anyway," responded Mr. Kim, the owner of Kim's Liquor Store, with a warming grin.

Jonny or Esther or both were in Mr. Kim's Liquor, Beer and Wine almost everyday of the week buying a bag of Takis or maybe a couple of scratch tickets but they would always buy beer. They had purchased beer that ranged from the aforementioned Miller High Life to Chimay depending on how much money was in either of their pockets.

"Thanks Mr. Kim see you tomorrow."

"See you Mr. Kim."

"Esther your shoe laces are untied. Estoy bromeando! They're not. Always tripping over some bull shit though."

"Shut the fuck up, puto! That's what you're going to do one-day watch, when you trip and fall and fuck yourself all up. No te estoy ayudando."

"I guess you were just looking out for me. But damn babe, I almost had to fuck you up," Jonny said jokingly as he kissed her forehead.

"Shit," laughed Esther. "I'll beat your ass boy. You know that."

Jonny and Esther walked the three blocks to Jonny's apartment hand in hand both of them clutching the black bag filled with beer. Excited about drinking their Tall Boys but more excited about drinking together. Jonny typed on his phone with his free hand.

That's how their relationship worked, one moment they were happy, they looked as if they were the most loving and together couple that relationships had ever seen. They made other couples in their company jealous of their companionship. They seemed to be the inspiration for every tragic couple owned by antiquity. But a seemingly innocent comment or gesture would turn into a Hellish war; a utopia would quickly descend into chaos. Both of their eyes would fill with hateful blood that could not know compromise. They would become bitter rivals, intense and destructive enemies, whose goal was not only to make one another submit unequivocally but to torture.

If Jonny did not wash the dishes after dinner, after many times of reminding Jonny, Esther's voice would become increasingly stern and vicious with every subsequent notice. Then Esther would lash out. Insidious words wrought from her tongue would be discharged from her dirty mouth aimed right at Jonny's heart. Jonny would begin to yell, Esther would yell louder. Then Esther would cry.

"Have you been washing some other bitches dishes or what? Limpie, perezoso puto! Yo cociné! So clean!"

"What the fuck are you talking about? I've washed the dishes like every night since I've known your fucking ass. What the fuck are you talking about? I'm going to wash them just calm the fuck down. As long as it gets done. I'm not washing any other bitches dishes. Where the fuck did you get that from? Oh, I know where your fucking ass!"

"Well, then wash them you fucking lazy ass bitch!"

Jonny was preoccupied with his phone that is why he would not do the dishes when Esther asked him. In fact, he probably did not hear Esther's first two hundred requests. His focus was on his phone. Esther then grabbed a red meat soiled knife from the sink and threw it at Jonny. Jonny hopped off of the couch and threw his phone on the bed. He then grabbed a sponge and began washing the dishes.

"Are you happy now? You are fucking mad!"

"You know you were going to let them sit all night. Yes I am fucking happy, asshole."

Esther and Jonny possessed a volatility that knew no compromise it had no filter or had any claim or stake in civility.

Esther came home thirty minutes late from work one night. As soon as she walked through the door Jonny chided her about supposed infidelities because she did not call and tell him that she would be late for dinner.

Jonny and Esther did not technically live together but Esther would always visit Jonny right after she got off of work to eat and shower and just rest with the love of her life. She would always spend the night. Jonny's love also had a key and much of her wardrobe littered the tile floors of Jonny's small studio apartment.

Esther had fallen off of her bike and scraped her knee that is why she was late.

"I'm home babe."

Jonny didn't answer. He just sat on the edge of the king sized bed that swallowed most of the room in the apartment.

"Where the fuck have you been and why is your fucking knee scraped? You're thirty minutes late so that means you were sucking dick for at least fifteen minutes because it only takes 15 minutes for you to bike it home from work. You fucking whore…"

"What the fuck is wrong with you Jonathan? I fell off of my fucking bike. Your fat ass never even rides yours anymore so you forgot what it feels like."

"You only get scraped knees from sucking cock. Your knees have been perfect for months and now they come home scraped? And I saw that text message in your phone too. Who is 'I Don't Know?' I know who it is. The name of the guy whose cock you just sucked!" yelled Jonny.

"You're a fucking idiot, estupido! I wish I did suck a big fat dick you fucking loser. I'm not a hoe like you. You are the biggest fucking puto," responded Esther.

"You wish you did? Huh, you fucking whore?"

"You're a whore you stupid lowlife asshole!"

Esther then charged at Jonny with an epic rage. Jonny turned to run away from her but Esther jumped on his back and pulled him to the ground by his face. Esther stood up and began to kick Jonny in his back and legs. Jonny lay on the ground; he cradled himself and protected his head from Esther's fury. Jonny laughed.

"Stop, laughing you fucking asshole. Cállate you little bitch!" Esther ordered.

"You're not doing shit to me. All you're doing is making your dumb ass tired! You dirty fucking whore!" Jonny expressed mockingly.

This only enraged Esther further as she jumped on top of Jonny and began to claw at his face. Jonny grabbed her wrists and turned her over, her back pressed against the cold tile.

"You want to hit me? Hit yourself! Hit yourself!"

Jonny had Esther by the wrists and Esther was hitting herself by his force. Esther knew that physically she was not stronger than Jonny but she couldn't admit to that fact. It wasn't hurtful, just very irritating.

"You see how easy this is for me? I am way stronger than your weak ass. Stop fucking with me. You don't want to fight me. You think you're stronger than me huh, slut?"

Then Jonny placed his hands around Esther's neck.

"I... can't... breathe..."

"Stop fucking with me! Who is 'I Don't Know?' I know you sucked his cock, didn't you? That's why you're fucking late bitch!"

"...Please!" Esther begged while gasping for air.

"Who the fuck is 'I Don't Know?' Who are you trying to hide? Why were you late coming home? Answer me!"

"I... am... sorry."

Jonny released his hands from around Esther's neck and then he kissed her on her forehead. Esther sits up and sobbingly kissed Jonny on his cheek. She then wrapped his left arm around her.

"You're fucking crazy, babe but I love you."

The entire fight lasted only about three minutes. Esther got home thirty minutes late at six in the evening it was now six o'three according to Jonny's phone. Which he happened to grab after he kissed Esther's forehead.

"So are you Bella. That was a crazy one huh? Is my face bleeding? But who is 'I Don't Know' Bella?"

"I don't know Jonathan. I never responded to their texts if you would have looked at it correctly, estupido. Here you can check my phone," Esther tossed Jonny her phone.

"This fight was loco pero the night we both almost got arrested was worse. I fucked you up that night. Let me see your face babe. Here in the light. Yeah you are bleeding on your cheek. Nothing you can't handle though babe. Lo siento but my neck fucking hurts..."

...

Turner and Ash were in town from San Diego for the weekend. They drove up because Turner had committed to an MBA conference at USC, which had just ended.

Jonny and Turner were in the backseat of Turner's car, taking turns drinking scotch from a flask, which was passed to Esther who sat shotgun whilst Ash drove them north on Figueroa into the heart of downtown.

"Turn right on 7th street," Jonny told Ash, "then make a left on Main. We should start looking for parking now. The bar we're going to is on 6th and Main."

The group arrived at The Association. Jonny sped to the restroom while the others went straight to the bar. Jonny returned and the women had drinks in their hands, Turner was still reviewing the menu.

"Jonny what's good here? I want some gin."

Jonny responded hastily, "The Antidote or the Last Word are pretty tasty. I've fucked with those two before but you can't go wrong with anything on the menu. I want some something Rye though… Bartender, how you doing tonight? Can I get an Avenue, please? You think you know what you want yet Turner?"

"Yeah, can I'll take an Antidote. Charge it!" Turner said as he pulled out his credit card, "I got this round Jonny."

"Good looking out… Esther, Ash? What did you two get?"

Ash had gotten a Mai Tai and Esther had just finished her Hemingway.

"Jonny can you get me another Hemingway please?"

It was early on a Friday evening. They, a seemingly bored couple who sat at the bar, and a DJ playing the greatest hits of the 1990's were the only people there that weren't staff. Two more drinks for both Turner and Ash, three more for Jonny, and four for Esther then they were off to Spring Street Bar.

…

"Lo siento Bella. I know I should trust you just like you trust me."

"I told you, babe. I only love you and you know that. Te amo. I am only a whore for you babe. I'll always be your whore, always."

"You will mi amor. I will always be your slut Bella. Te amo tambien, mucho, mucho. It's just weird when you come home late. I worry that something horrible may have happened to you, like you could have died, and when I see you come through that door in good health, I fucking fear the worst. I think you're fucking someone else or something."

"Ay, babe! You're so cute. Why were you checking my shit though? When did you check my phone?"

"When you were in the shower this morning. I saw you received a text and I just took a peek at your home screen that's all. I'll fuck 'I Don't Know' up!"

"I know you would you fucking psycho. ¿Crees que los vecinos nos oyeron?"

"No they didn't, shhh I'm reading."

The neighbors always heard Ester and Jonny fighting. Jonny continued to go through all the text messages that "I Don't Know" had sent Esther. Esther did not reply to any of them. Jonny was relieved. At least until he started to comprehend what he was reading.

"Why the fuck would this person say 'Your pussy was great last night?' Why the fuck would he send that? That text was sent three months ago! What does this text say? 'I can't wait to fuck you again!' Esther you better explain this shit right fucking now! I fucking knew it! I always knew it! You dirty fucking tramp bitch! Fuck that! You have to get the fuck out of my apartment right fucking now! Please just go right fucking now. Before I fucking go crazy."

...

Jonny, Esther, Ash, and Turner left The Association and walked over to Spring Street Bar. It was crowded; luckily as the group entered another was leaving and they grabbed four seats. Jonny stood up from the table and headed towards the bathroom. After a few minutes he came back to the table and took drink orders.

"I'm headed to the bar. What do you all want?"

As he took Esther, Ash, and Turner's orders a young woman who had just left the restroom herself brushes against Jonny's back.

"Excuse me baby."

"You're excused… So you want a Gin and Tonic Turner, Ash you don't want anything else because you're driving and Esther you said you wanted a Whiskey Sour…"

"I don't want anything Jonathan. I'm done for the night."

"Are you sure? We're just getting started. What happened?"

"I told you that I don't want anything," Esther said as she pulled out her phone.

"I'll order a drink for you then. If you don't drink it, I'll drink it."

"Do whatever the fuck you want," said Esther as Jonny walked to the bar.

Unbeknownst to him he stood next to the woman who brushed up against him. Jonny had his hand raised to get the bartender's attention but he was busy with other customers.

...

"Stop, Jonathan! Stop! I have never ever cheated on you. Yo prometo babe. I promise you. I have no clue who that fucking person is. I never ever read the texts from that number. I don't know how to block numbers on my phone so I just left it alone. I have no clue why that loser keeps texting me. I'm not responding. I never respond."

"Why have you been trying to hide this from me? You must have something to hide."

"I don't babe. Someone must be playing a joke on me. I promise you babe. I promise I only want you and love you. I've only fucked you since we've known each other."

"Well I'm about to text this motherfucker and you better pray that it is some clown playing a joke because on your life you'll be dead."

"And when I'm right I'm going to fucking kill you for putting me through this."

"What the fuck would you think if you saw some texts like 'I love the way your cock tastes' or some bull shit in my phone? What the fuck would you think?"

"I would fuck you up and you know I would."

"Well… then let me text this motherfucker and I hope you're praying to someone. You motherfucking…"

"I'm tired of you calling me a slut and a whore."

"I almost did that time. I'm going to save calling you a slut and a whore and even worse for after this fucking asshole's response."

...

Jonny's arm got tired so he put it down and pulled out his phone. The woman who had called him baby in front of Esther yelled to Jonny over the loud Thelonious Monk recording, "This place is too fucking crowded. All I want is a goddamn drink. Can they please hire more bartenders?"

"I can't hear you, I'm sorry. What did you say?"

"They need to hire more bartenders," the woman yelled into Jonny's ear.

"That would be helpful. I think I'm sobering up I've been waiting so fucking long. Don't they know the drunker I am the more money I spend, the larger their fucking tip?"

The woman laughed and flirtatiously hit Jonny on his shoulder as he typed on his phone.

"What the fuck is the hold up? I'm getting me a fucking drink right now."

Jonny pushed his way to the front of the bar, the young woman followed.

"We should have done that earlier."

"I know I should have. This is fucking nonsense."

Esther sat at their table and watched Jonny interact with this woman. She sat unflappable and resigned. She laughed at Turner's jokes and was able to hold an endeared conversation with Ash without revealing the anger, which had been festering inside of her since that woman bumped into Jonny.

Eventually, Jonny returned to the table with Turner's Gin and Tonic, a Bulleit Rye neat, and a Racer 5 for Esther.

"Jonathan, Abigail is outside and we're going to a bar in Hollywood. Can you walk me outside please?" Esther told Jonny as she put her phone in her purse.

"What the fuck? Are you fucking with me? You're fucking serious? When did this happen? I thought we were hanging out tonight? You did not tell me that you were even thinking about hanging out with Abigail tonight."

...

Jonny first typed a text to "I Don't Know" inquiring about this person's true identity. "I Don't Know" responded right away. The months of not receiving a response made this person very anxious it seemed. Jonny typed a second text that asked how the mysterious texter got Esther's phone number. The answer to that text made Jonny visibly upset. He looked up from the phone and stared at Esther sadistically. He then typed a third text.

...

"I swear you never mentioned this to me," Jonny told Esther as they walked out of the bar and onto Spring Street.
"Who the fuck was that bitch you were talking to at the bar?" Esther asked and before Jonny could answer Esther punched him in the nose then ran across the street. An infuriated and enraged Jonny started to run after her but blood began to rush from his nose and onto his clothes, his pursuit halted in the middle of Spring Street. He ran back into the bar covering his nose, rushing passed Ash and Turner, who were still at the table, to the bathroom.
"What the fuck is up with that clown?" Turner asked Ash.

...

Jonny wanted to lure this person out of hiding so he could confront him face to face and pummel Esther's possible Sancho. After reading the response Jonny felt relieved and tossed Esther back her phone.
"Sorry about that babe. I cooked dinner and it's ready, so let's eat."
"What the fuck did it say you goddamn asshole? I told you I would never ever cheat on you babe. Nunca, nunca, nunca!"
"Read it!"
Esther read "I Don't Know's" last text.

...

A bloody right handprint stained the bathroom mirror; the water ran whilst Jonny's left hand massaged his nose that dripped like a broken faucet.

"I can't believe she made me bleed. Fuck that bitch… What the fuck was she talking about? I didn't talk to any bitch in front of her… I'm supposed to be rude? I'm supposed to not respond when spoken to? No woman can ever talk to me for the rest of my life?
I'm really going to get some broads phone number in front her? Fuck my nose hurts! I'm never talking to her bitch ass ever a-fucking-gain." Jonny punched the soap dispenser, "She really ruined my favorite shirt. This bitch really made me bleed…" Jonny then punched the electric paper towel dispenser; it wouldn't stop dispensing paper towels, the roll coiled around Jonny's legs. "That bitch better not talk to me ever again! She better not say a goddamn thing to me! Stupid ass bitch! I can't even breathe out of my motherfucking nose!"

As Jonny raised his fist to his reflection in the mirror partially covered by stray bloody handprints, his phone rang.

"Where the fuck are you Jonathan? You're really going to let me stand at the bus stop all-alone, all by myself at this time of night? You fucking pussy bitch! You better come wait with me right-fucking-now! Or else Jonathan, or else!"

"Bitch, you must be out of your goddamn mind. I'm bleeding all over the fucking place because of you, over some bull shit!" Jonny left the bathroom and up to Turner and Ash who were still at the table.

"I have to go see what's up with Esther, have a safe drive back to San Diego bro."

Turner and Jonny shook hands, Jonny took the phone from his chest then ran out of Spring Street Bar.

"What-fucking-bus stop are you at?"

"You better be on your fucking way Jonathan!"

"What-fucking bus stop are you at? Goddamn it! Answer my fucking question. Listen, fucking listen for a goddamn change!"

"Where else would I be Jonathan? Use your fucking mind, your stupid ass whore obsessed brain; we catch the '30' to Boyle Heights, don't we? Where is the nearest '30' bus stop? Broadway and Fifth you fucking bitch! You're the fucking bitch, bitch!"

"Goddamn it, I fucking hate you! You fucking slut bitch!"

...

"That's fucking funny! El pensaba que yo era un prostitute he fucked in Atlantic City? That asshole. He thinks I'm a whore too," Esther chuckles. "I've only been on a plane once babe, that one trip we took to visit your family."

"I know Bella, too fucking funny. He almost made me kill you. That would have been a huge mistake," Jonny said indifferently.

"I don't know why you think you could kill me. Like I said 'I will fuck you up boy.' Don't fuck with me."

...

Esther punched and scratched; each punched hit a wrist or the back of a palm as Jonny covered his head. When Jonny covered his head she then directed blows at his body. Any pain she could inflict she would. She distressed Jonny's shirts then ripped it, as his shirt tore down the middle of the collar Esther's nails dug deep into his skin.

"Fuck you Jonathan! Go be with that bitch! Why are you waiting with me at the bus stop? Your bitch is going to be mad! Didn't she give you her number? And you took that shit? You took it happily too, Jonathan, happily. You fucking whore ass bitch! Right in front of me too you have no respect for me you motherfucking bitch." Esther kept punching, grabbing, and clawning.

"Esther, you better calm the fuck down right now. I'm trying my hardest not to knock your dumb ass."

Jonny then grabbed Esther around her neck. His hands wrapped like a noose Esther still clawed and punched until she eventually had to deal with her loss of breath.

"Let... me... go..."

"I told you to stop fucking with me! I didn't get any bitche's number! I haven't done shit you dumb ass bitch! Say you're fucking sorry! Say you're sorry for breaking my nose. Tell me your fucking sorry or you're dying... right fucking now."

"I... I... I'm... I'm sor... I'm sorry."

Jonny let go and dropped his arms.

Esther was still not intimidated. Tears manifested in her eyes.

"How are you going to leave me for that bitch?" She then continued her assault. "Fuck that bitch and fuck you too, Jonathan. You're going to regret choosing that ugly bitch over me."

Jonny didn't choke Esther to subdue her this time he grabbed her wrists and focused his eyes on hers.
"Fuck that bitch and fuck you! She started talking to me. I didn't get her phone number. I didn't do a goddamn thing but order drinks for us. You're going insane for no goddamn reason! Don't make me fuck you up out here,"

Jonny then took Esther's left hand and made it hit her face, "You see how much stronger I am than you? I will fuck you up!" Jonny took her right hand and did the same; Esther seemed defeated, "Stop fucking with me! Bye Esther, it's fucking over!"

Jonny violently dropped Esther's arms and as soon as he turned his back to her he saw a Los Angeles Police

Department squad car that was heading south on Broadway make a U-Turn and shine a light into his eyes. Without hesitation or direction Jonny turned around and put his hands on the steel shutter door of the Ramirez Cake Shop.

"Get the fuck out of here officer. This isn't none of your fucking business. We're good kids," Esther told the over zealous officer who was placing Jonny in handcuffs.

"By the looks of this fellow you need to go to jail too." An officer then ordered Esther's hands behind her back and put her in handcuffs.

"Now you both are going to jail."

"What the fuck for? I can't argue with my woman, my love?"

...

"Just sit down and eat Flaca, damn! I know you would babe."

"Since you've been in my phone all night let me see your fucking phone. See who have you been texting. Let me see what bitches have been texting you."

"Fuck no!"

One Last Sunday

Jonny and his two friends were in a cab heading south on Chicago Street.

"Right here. Stop right here. Right in front," Jonny told the driver.

The cab driver stopped in front of Saint Mary's Church.

"Let me borrow two hundred bucks David?" asked Jonny.

"Sure brother, here."

David handed him eight twenties, two tens, and four five-dollar bills. All of the cash he had in his wallet, one hundred twenty-dollars of which was from Jonny From a trick-shout bet he had won at the pool hall earlier.

"I'll see you both tonight."

"Yeah, Jonny we'll see you. Make sure you're at the airport on time," responded Amanda.

Jonny, David and Amanda had been celebrating an anniversary and they were going to continue celebrating later that night in their hometown of Seattle. The occasion was somber as it had always been. The fourth to their trio had been dead for ten years on this particular Sunday morning.

"I can't believe it's been ten fucking years man."

"Ten years... I still feel seventeen. I haven't matured one-fucking-bit since then," admitted Jonny.

"Those are the truest words you have ever spoke," David commented smugly, "Just don't be late Jonny. Get to the fucking airport."

"Calm the Hell down. I'll be there, David. Fuck..." Jonny then sighed, "I said I'll see you both tonight and I will. I've never missed this night."

"Why do you have to do this, why are you going to this church? Stay in the cab. We can wait for you to pack then we can head to the airport together," Amanda urged.

"Your flight is three hours before mine... This is for Stasee. I feel like I have to do this. I think it'll help me and I think it will help her too."

"Well, good luck, man."

"Yeah, good luck Jonny. I know it's been awhile." David wished as the cab's door slammed.

His longtime best friends remained in the yellow taxi, which made a U-turn and headed west down Fourth Street to their downtown Los Angeles hotel.

It had been quite a long time since Jonny had been to Sunday morning service. He wasn't religious and that's why he wasn't an atheist. God sort of existed to him but he would always qualify his belief by saying, "If my God exists then she's evil as fuck!" Never definitively declaring that there is a God, being, or plain of existence greater than this earth, in the United States of America, state of California, city of Los Angeles, neighborhood of Boyle Heights, on Chicago Street standing in front of Saint Mary's Church on Sunday morning. He would simply admit to the existence of the idea.

"If God does exist then how does humanity absolve terror and horror? How do people forgive malevolence and malignance and its motives? Prayer? Confession? Do you believe in a God that created everything? Look at all that she has created. Look at everything. Not just the fucking flowers and the kittens and all of the pretty shit. Look at the gritty shit. God created the ultimate purveyor of 'evil' Satan."

Jonny didn't understand prayer or confession or how religious people found it good for their souls. He liked to yell and scream, cry and fight. He was violent in his catharsis, he purged not through prayer but with visceral feats, self-mutilating actions against his body and his mind. He only understood how he perceived the universe and knew that there is no being that is All Good, indomitably benevolent. Jonny also understood that what was true for him most likely wasn't true for anyone else. He also thought that most people were imbecilic, something he also knew he was.

If you disregard the inconvenience of funerals; friend's deaths, the death of relatives, friend's of relatives, relative's of relatives, people he had never seen before but attended their wake because a friend needed his support, people he had no connection to at all, watching every casket close vapidly, unable to assess the weight of death because the lifeless body in the casket didn't, Jonny had not been inside of a church for eleven years, if not for funerals and an inability to ignore death, Jonny would have never stepped foot in a church.

"I would probably burn this church to the ground if your cousin wasn't lying in that casket," Jonny said to his friend Willie after a car hit Willie's cousin whilst he was riding his motorcycle.

"It feels weird in here."

He felt obligated to pay his respects to the dead. The lives led and listen to a priest and the deceased's family taut the life of the poor sap in the casket. Knowing that the person dead, most often, had lived the life of an asshole.

Jonny's first Sunday morning service in eleven years, he had refused to listen to a priest exude Christ's lessons and preach the benefits of God all-the-while almost completely absolving human indecency especially, the unseemliness that resides behind the walls of the Catholic Church and all other denominations of Christianity. All he saw was the religious elitism that denied any other possibility of creation or living, any other possibility of faith. He couldn't understand how people quarreled over religion when all of their confessed believes seemed equally plausible, meaning, not likely.

"You can steal your mom's car and drive it to your grandma's house to rape her butt and as long as you repent, you're forgiven? That's bullshit!"

Jonny never wanted to hear ever again how God and Jesus and her Spirit could only do good in your life and only make you do good.

At first it was a conscious decision not to attend church. By the time he finished high school he forgot that he used to go to church at least once a week since birth. It wasn't a habit he had developed, not to attend, it just happened. Jonny had stayed in bed until at least three in the afternoon every Sunday morning since Stasee's death. He became an every Saturday night social drinker the year before; an every night drinker currently. Refusing to attend church a year earlier because of what was happening to Stasee there.

Jonny wore nice black slacks, a neat but beer stained white and black striped blouse, black suspenders, and a double Winsor knot in his solid black wrinkled tie; he looked as if he had just came from a wild wedding reception, as he entered the church. Despite his ruffled clothing and distraught disposition Jonny still looked dapper, much more desirable than his typically grungy appearance.

The tone of that morning was of another funeral. Jonny's disposition was glum and gloomy, sullen, it tritely mirrored the foggy and grey December Boyle Heights overcast. His eyes were a crimson red, like blood stains after they set in bright cloth. He smelled of all the tenants of a bar in the nineteen nineties before they banned cigarettes; tobacco smoke, alcohol and desperation.

Jonny would never dress well for church; church would never be worth the occasion. The night before Jonny's daunting visit, Amanda, David and Jonny did what they did every anniversary of Stasee's death. They would drink until they could forget that she was dead. They could never forget so they never stopped drinking. Another Saturday night and La Gonzales' State Street Billiards had once again taken all of Jonny's money. Only this night Margarita and Luis the owners allowed them to stay and drink passed recognition of California's liquor laws. Margarita called a cab for them at 7:45 in the morning.

Although, Amanda and David had a strong affinity for Stasee they obviously loved her and knew that it was impossible to quantify their love for her, Jonny loved Stasee unwillingly. It pained him to love her even when she was alive. He had always loved her and always understood that he could never-not love a person as entrancing as she. And in the ten years since she passed he still possessed the same adulation and yearning. She was his best friend, a woman who he would love his entire life regardless of girlfriend, wife or mistress. Jonny would only ditch his stained and ripped denim shorts faded black t-shirts, and skullcaps for Stasee. All of those funerals and she was the only occasion.

"This is for you," Jonny whispered to himself upon entering the church. The pews were a dark brown oak covered with blue cushions that also matched the carpet. The sanctuary was dimly lit, illuminated by the sun's rays who attempted to peer through the deep gray clouds trying desperately to reach the praying saints on the sanctuary's stained glass windows. The room smelled of perfume and cologne as if God mandated that the church parishioners smelled like flowers and dress just as colorful. All of which became very sensitive to Jonny's sleepless and inebriated senses. It was about 8:15 in the morning and the congregation at Saint Mary's church was greeting and situating themselves, anxiously awaiting the priest to address them.

Jonny sat down in the last pew of the middle section and put his head in his hands.
He sat remembering despite his earlier attempts to paralyze his memory. He was still forlorn and sorrowful because he should have never had to dress nicely. He hated it. He wanted

to tear off his clothing and burn them; he wanted to use the oak pews as kindling. He kept Stasee with him everyday but on the anniversary of her death it was the day she jumped off of the Aurora Bridge all over again.

    Stasee jumping off that bridge wanting to die, sure that her life had to be over. Forgetting her best friends and Jonny and her mother and her sisters and her baby brother and her future. Not understanding that she was apart of them like they were a part of her. Taking her life simply because it was hers and if that sick nun didn't want it she didn't want it either.

    Stasee left a suicide note. She left it in Jonny's bedroom the night before she left forever. They were 17 year olds up late watching their favorite movie, *Boogie Nights*, in Jonny's bedroom. Jonny's mother loved Stasee and Stasee's parents Jonny. Since they were young kids in Ms. Gardener's kindergarten class or Mr. Gomes' 7th grade science class or Mrs. Chavez English class their sophomore year of high school, they would spend the night at each other's homes. They ate lunch together and walked each other home from school. They went camping and drank their first beer together. At 15 they got drunk for the first time together. Stasee even tried out for the football team with Jonny until one day he had to go up against Stasee in tackling drills. They both walked away and never returned to the football field. They watched pornography and sports and smoked their first joint together. They both loved film.

    "I love you Jonny. You're going to be a beautiful man," She said to Jonny right before William H. Macy kills his porn star wife played by real life porn star Nina Hartley.

    "You're going to be the most beautifulest woman. I can't wait to see where we'll be in ten years," Jonny reciprocated as William H. Macy walked despondent from the bedroom and puts the gun to his own mouth. To Jonny, Stasee already was the most beautiful woman on the planet.

He didn't find the letter until he came home from the hospital that Monday morning. Stasee had placed in-between the pages of their eighth grade yearbook from Tilamook Middle School, which they had looked through earlier that week. Jonny never told anyone she wrote one, in fact he destroyed it the day of her wake. But he remembered the letter, every dreadful word.

The priest had not yet begun his sermon. Jonny was nervously scanning the congregation, searching for his girlfriend, Esther. Also, he had to note where the ushers were stationed so he knew when he could take a swig from his flask. Which he discovered in the front left pocket of his pants getting out of the cab.

Esther attended mass most Sundays and never bothered to invite Jonny because it was difficult to wake him up and because she didn't want to hear any of his demonizing protests of the Catholic Church and of religion in general.

"They only want to control your money and to control what you do so they can control more of your money," is what Jonny would say to Esther while he was half asleep.

"Why is your church the nicest fucking building in the neighborhood? It looks better than the damn hospital for fuck sakes and twenty times better than the damn high school."

His favorite line. When he said that Esther scurried out of the apartment quickly because she knew she wasn't going to shut him up for at least 45 minutes.
She'd leave then Jonny would fall back asleep and remain asleep until she returned home.

"¡Bienvenidos al la gente! Dios a hecho otro día hermoso!" the priest began his sermon.

"Dios es gran, verdad? Quiero hablar con ustedes acerca del perdón. El perdón de Dios. Y como pudieran obtener su perdon? Sin importar el delito ó la vergüenza que pueden ser redimidos. Todo lo que tienen que hacer es arrepentirse y hacer uso de su alma a nuestro gran Dios…"

Jonny sat in quiet respite, still in back of the sanctuary head in his hands mourning what he was about to do, what he was about to say in this dreaded holy place. He knew that Stasee would disapprove because she was non-confrontational and a sweetheart, Jonny's antithesis. She understood and she believed in God and God's promises. She loved the church and was thoroughly involved in coordinating events for the teens in the congregation, many of them she had known since grade school at Tiffany Lake; Jonny, David and Amanda her closest friends since then. Jonny would soon discover why Stasee loved church and loved staying after service to help the nuns, who always seemed to insist that she do so.

The priest continued "…En Mateo dice, 'Porque si perdonáis a los hombres sus ofensas, vuestro Padre celestial os perdonará a vosotros. Pero si no perdonáis a los hombres sus ofensas, tampoco vuestro Padre os perdonará vuestras ofensas.' Versículo 6."

Jonny still sitting in the back of the sanctuary head down and spinning, feeling a bit nauseous from all of the drinks he had had last night and this morning, sick from another anniversary, this needless commemoration. He had only eaten two tacos since David and Amanda came into town and Margarita at La Gonzales' Billiards forced him to eat them.

"Está pálido, Jonathan. ¡Coma hijo!" She told him.

He tried to shut out the priest's words but couldn't help but absorb all that he was preaching. He listened and groaned at every piercing and seething word drawing mild attention for the patrons seated in the back row pews.

"Crean en el perdón de Dios. Sin embargo, algunas personas se niegan a perdonar a sí mismos. Dios no puede perdonar si no perdonan a sí mismo. Juan dice: 'Si confesamos nuestros pecados, él es fiel y justo para perdonar nuestros pecados, y limpiarnos de toda maldad.' Versículo 1. Confiese sus pecados y perdonar a sí mismo y luego nuestro maravilloso Dios te perdonará también…"

The night before Jonny, David and Amanda had frequented La Gonzales' State Street Billiards on First Street and State. It was Jonny's favorite hang out in the neighborhood because he could play pool and they had cheap drinks, $2.50 per beer. As Jonny told it to all of his friends who he persuaded to the brightly lit, foggy from cigarette smoke, dank, cash only Paisa bar, "You can get 2 beers for 5 bucks!"

David and Amanda didn't mind where they were going they just wanted to get blitzed for as cheap as possible. It was their final night in Los Angeles before they flew back to Seattle and drinking with Jonny wasn't cheap no matter the price of the beer. They had already gone over their spending budget for the trip.

"8 ball side pocket, bitch," confidently chided Jonny as the pool cue glided smoothly between the backside of his left palm and thumb.

"You missed! You fucking suck, dick head." said Amanda as she lined up her next shot.

"Count how many balls you have left on the table. You're trash Mandy."

"Yeah, one more than you have baby nuts."

Amanda made her next two shots, she was stripes.

"I let you catch up. You're not making this shit!"

"Off the wall, 8 ball corner pocket." Amanda walks around the table to ensure she has the angles to make the mildly difficult shot.

"Yeah fucking right. You're not making that shit. Hurry up and shoot!"

The cue ball bounced off the right wall and hit the 8 Ball, which was about seven inches from the left corner pocket. She made it and it looked easy.

"You lose again Jonny. You fucking loser, another round on you."

"You motherfuckers are doctors and I always have to pay. Fuck you two. You aren't ever going to drive my Ferrari."

"Now Jonny that's not nice. We let you drive ours last week… Broke asshole. Go get us our drinks," said David as he gave Amanda a celebratory kiss.

None of them had a Ferrari.

"Next time I'm going to come pick you two up from the airport on my handle bars. Don't fuck with me. I'll be right back, I have to take a piss."

Jonny threw his pool cue on the table and headed towards the restroom. When he entered he saw an older man about retirement age, 5'7", darker complexion, wearing a pair of Lee jeans and a snakeskin belt. He had placed his Tejana on the paper towel dispenser and began doing lines of coke that he had already cut off of the restroom sink with a short straw.

"Nothing wrong with a little nose candy," boldly admitted Jonny.

The man looked at Jonny through the mirror as Jonny unzipped his pants in front of the lone urinal in the bathroom. The door had been taken off of the stall of the only toilet. When he went to wash his hands the man was putting a small pouch of cocaine and a straw into the left pocket of his shirt.

"Es verdad. Nothing wrong with a little nose candy. If you or your friends necesitas. Yo tengo. I'm at the bar."

The man patted Jonny on his back then walked out of the bathroom. Jonny washed his hands and then dried them on his Calvin Klein slacks and headed straight to the bar to buy another round for David, Amanda, and himself.

"Otra ronda, bonita. Tres botellas de Negra Modelo"

"Si, mijo. Limón, verdad?"

"Dos con limón. Yo no quiero. Gracias Margarita."

The bartender knew Jonny well. He was one of her many regulars and stood out more than most because he was the youngest. Most of the patrons who frequented State Street Billiards were older men and woman who just wanted cheap beer and a place wear they could smoke their cigarettes and cigars indoors or they were Cholos and Cholas who had lived through the gang wars of the nineteen nineties. Jonny's generation usually hung out downtown or at the new dive bar across the street.

Margarita was an older woman, about 66 years old from a small town in Nayarit, México. She and her husband Luis had owned La Gonzales Billiards since 1984.

"Here you go clowns. Let's go again Amanda. You keep getting fucking lucky! I swear," remarked Jonny as he sipped his beer.

"I want to play against David now. I'm tired of kicking your ass."

"I play winner then."

"Duh, Jonny. Cocksucker."

Jonny downed the rest of his beer and placed it on top of the pyramid of beer bottles that the three of them had manufactured. At the base was ten Modelo and Negra Modelo bottles; Jonny added the sixth beer to the third row as Margarita walked over with a bottle of Tequila, three shots already poured.

"Disfrutan niños."

"Gracias Margarita, Gracias. Hey Amanda, David? Take a shot with me."

David made a toast, "To Stasee. The most beautiful person we'll ever know."

They clinked their shot glasses together, pounded them on the pool table's pine and then down the hatch.

"That was fucking harsh! They serve hard liquor here? What time does this dump close?" inquired David.

"Mamá Lucia tequila. So fucking good. She only serves it to her regulars. It's from her hometown in México. And the doors close at two in the morning. Hey man, this is my bar don't be talking shit. And come on and break already. Jesus Fucking H Christ."

Jonny's head was still down in the back of the church. But instead of his hands supporting his head he had his hands over his ears as if each syllable was an incendiary grenade designed specifically to destroy how he thought.

The priest recurrently, "Y cuando estéis orando, si tienen algo contra alguien, perdónalo, por lo que su Padre que está en los cielos os perdone a vosotros vuestras ofensas."

"Purple, side pocket." Jonny was on his game now. He was once again playing Amanda who had beaten David. David was at the bar purchasing another round.

"Blue ball, corner pocket..." Jonny continued to clear the table. Amanda stood there, pool cue in her right hand and beer in the other.

"You only have one ball and it's blue! You just have it bad all around don't you Jonny." Amanda slapped him on his back firmly as he went to take the shot.

As Jonny missed, "Do you still remember Stasee's favorite poem, Jonny? When she was upset she would recite it to herself.
I remember the first time I caught her whispering it under her breath. We were running for the school bus the same day her

lizard, Arthur, had died. She wanted to stay home from school desperately but her parents wouldn't let her because it was 'just a lizard'. At least that's what she had come to understand. That was their way of consoling her, diminishing its importance. 'You're going to learn that a lizard is only a lizard'. They would tell her. But she disagreed. She knew it wasn't and was inconsolable. She loved that lizard and its death couldn't be understood. The bus had already left and I remember Stasee whispering it to herself, tears swelling in her already swollen eyes;

'All is well in life I'll see.
I'm above ground and I can breathe.
Trials can't last forever.
Or nothing could be defined clever.
Apart of life trials must become.
Don't let sadness make you dumb.'

She then ran as fast as she could to the next bus stop. The bus driver noticed her determination and waited for her. I was not too far behind and we made it to school on time. She was an incredible girl. Fuck I miss her. "

"Yeah, I remember that poem… And you know what? Fuck that fucking poem! I love her but fuck that fucking poem! I fucking hate it. Fuck her and that fucking poem. 'Don't let sadness make you dumb?' I can't help it! Her stupid ass gave up on life and for what? What the fuck! Fuck her! Fuck this fucking day! I'm tired of it! We shouldn't be celebrating or commemorating or whatever this shit fucking day at all. She should fucking be here!" excitedly and loudly confessed Jonny. He then he took a swig from the bottle Mamá Lucia's that was half empty.

"Whatever Jonny... It's your fucking shot. None of us can help it! Stop mourning her life and live yours. You have so much potential but you let all of these excuses get in your fucking way. You always have a fucking excuse. Stasee loved us and we loved her but stop mourning her life. Celebrate the fuck out of it Jonny! For God sake you piece of fucking shit! Be angry with yourself. Don't ever be mad at her, ever! You dumb fuck!"

Amanda threw her pool cue on the table disorienting the game. Then she ran passed the narco, Margarita at the bar, and the three mariachis tuning their guitars and staring at the only television; crying.

"Damn she didn't have to start crying like a little bitch, Davey. Did she?"

"Shut the fuck up Jonny before I kick your fucking ass. You need to calm the fuck down. This is a fucking celebration. It always has been."

"But this is the day of her... whatever David. You're fucking right... Amanda is right too. Go get her please tell her to come back in. I'm sorry. I'm very fucking sorry. Come back and drink. Come on. This is a fucking celebration. I'm sorry. I still don't know how to deal with this shit. It's still fucking hard man. I miss her. I miss her a-whole-fucking-lot, everyday."

"We miss her everyday too. So does her mother and sisters and baby brother. It is fucking hard for all of us. You fucking know it is. That's why we still celebrate this day and her fucking birthday. We live for her every-damn-motherfucking day too, Jonny. This isn't about you being fucking angry with her. We all wish she was still here. And if that perverted fuck didn't... Let me go get Amanda. Please, just calm the fuck down and re-rack. Me and you are going to play."

David was successful in getting Amanda to rejoin the trio at the table.

"Amanda I'm sorry. I love you but…"

Amanda interrupted, "I understand Jonny. It's okay. I know."

The bar closed their doors at 1:45 in the morning. Margarita was still serving drinks and talking to the narco as the three mariachis began to play "Alma Enamorada" on their guitars.

"Don't we have to leave Jonny? Don't the doors close at two?" asked David.

"Not for us and not tonight."

Game after game of pool until it just became a trick shot competition, shot after shot of Mamá Lucia, two and a half bottles, and a second pyramid of Modelos. They even took the narco up on the offer he had made to Jonny earlier in the restroom.

Story after story about Stasee and her heart and who she was and who should could have been, filled the morning with her intelligence and her ingenuity and determination. All of the things that the group was incapable of after all of the drinking they had done.

That night weighed upon Jonny, mourning his friend's death and mourning what he was about to do. Wondering if Esther and her mother were in the congregation. Hoping he got to say everything he wanted to say before he was tackled and rushed out of the sanctuary by the ushers. Regardless, Jonny was still going to do what he came to Saint Mary's church that Sunday morning to do. Jonny drank from his flask.

Loudly the priest exclaimed, "Hechos versículo 3: 'Arrepentídos, pues, y se recomienden a Dios, para que vuestros pecados sean borrados, que tiempos de refrigerio vengan de parte del Señor.' Admitan sus errores y seran perdonados."

"Admit your wrongs!" Jonny yelled from the back of the sanctuary.

"¿Quien esta hablando?" inquired the priest. "¿Que han dicho?

"Admit your wrongs!" Jonny yelled again as he stood up and walked into the aisle.

"You fucking assholes! You moral monsters. You deplorable pieces of human shit! Admit that you're wrong! You don't believe what you say. No one here believes you or themselves."

The two ushers in the back of the church and two ushers from the sides rushed towards Jonny.

"¡Paren!" The priest ordered of the ushers. ""Que hable, está bien."

"You better let me speak you piece of shit! You've been speaking this bullshit for centuries. Let someone else have a turn. The church, the purveyor of all morality. How could you let her do that to her? Your vow of celibacy is a crock and my dead friends abused pussy is evidence of that. Why does your doctrine allow for that to happen to someone so beautiful, so pure, so perfect? Why are you charged with administering faith? Who the fuck is God to allow that to happen? She believed in God's word. She believed that Sister Sarah was showing her who she was. But she was only using her! To absolve her own sexual frustration. Your denial of God's nature. An evil woman spawned in this dark sadistic place you call a sanctuary for holiness and peace. You deplorable, despicable, lying sacks of shit! You awful mother…"

"Shut the fuck up Jonathan! ¡Cállate!" yelled a voice from the congregation. It was Jonny's girlfriend Esther.

"Esther you shut the fuck up! I already told you about coming to this damned building. Shut the fuck up! Priest, your God molested my best friend and then killed her. Despite her devotion to her fallacy, despite an unrelenting and unwavering belief in the lies she tells you to spew. She killed her. She let that demoness devour her pussy and forced her to take the cock of a devilish priest. A priest in a robe just like yours. Lauding those same words of forgiveness. You are her crooked messenger. You shall burn for your betrayal of humanity and decency… for your manipulation…"

"Jonathan te voy a chingar! ¡Cállate, Jonathan! ¡Estás en la iglesia!" pleaded Esther.

"…And she loved it and she loved you. She made her cum and blessed her and made her feel better than she ever could feel and then she killed her. Why did she do that? Why did God kill her? Why did Stasee love her and you? You aren't shit! Fuck you! Fuck this church and fuck God! Fuck that dyke nun and fuck that depraved priest! God doesn't believe in forgiveness! God hates us all, that's why he makes dumb asses like you all sit here on Sundays and listen to this bull shit! God is a pervert and a scam artist. She tells you what not to do and then abuses the lives of the youth. Fuck her! Stupid fucking cunt of a God!"

Jonny was then hit in the head with a Bible. Esther also threw one of her high heels at him.

"¡Sal de aquí ahora!" Esther had then ran from her seat at the front of the church towards Jonny and pushed him towards the cathedral doors. Not before slapping him in the face several times.

"Get the fuck out of here Jonathan! Right now and I'm not playing around. ¡Vamos puto!"

Esther attempted to contain Jonny as he continued to yell at the priest.

"God doesn't love us. God doesn't love you. He hates you! You suck the cocks of little fucking boys, you sell them hope then you rape little girls, you vile piece of garbage! You lick their little pussies. You supreme sodomite! You will never be forgiven! Fuck God! Fuck her promises and her pretention. She can't exist if she let you fucking assholes rule over her word. Unless that was her plan. To molest the world into believing her."

"Jonathan get the fuck out of here, right now. Please Jonathan? Don't make me fuck you up in front of the church and my mom and you know I will. I know you're upset and I know what today is but go home and go get ready. Get the fuck out here! You're embarrassing yourself. ¡Vives aqui! Estos son sus vecinos."

"Fuck God and fuck you, fuck all of you who listen and accept and believe and live this bullshit! Fuck you, fuck you, fuck you, fuck you and fuck God! Fuck her!"

Those were Jonny's final words inside of the church as Esther pushed him to the Chicago street curb.

"¿Que estas haciendo? ¿Eres estúpido o que? I know that you miss your friend and that's something I won't understand but you have to handle it better. Don't come to my church talking that bullshit. I accept it. I love you for how you think but she died. El sacerdote que mató a tu amigo fue put in prison. He's gone. No más. So is that nun. They weren't transferred they were put in prison. They've been punished. Dios no es responsable. It was them."

"Fuck you Esther. I'm out of here. FUCK GOD! THAT FUCKING TRAITOR LYING PIECE OF SHIT! Stasee loved her and God betrayed her."

Jonny then handed Esther the two hundred dollars that David had given to him an hour or so earlier.

"Give this to God for me. Tell her to kill herself. I'll call you when I get to the airport."

"Dame un beso estupido. Llamame." Esther ordered then she walked back into the church and as she found her seat next to her mother the priest joking remarked, "¿Hay un diablo en todos, verdad? Algunos más que otros. Y nosotros lo perdonamos por interrumpir la Palabra de Dios." The congregation erupted in laughter.

Jonny angrily walked home to his apartment on 4th Street and Saint Louis a block away from Saint Mary's Church. Into apartment 18 he went, a studio, where he threw himself onto the king size bed that took up more than half of the apartment's space. Head in his pillow he sobbed like Stasee when she lost her lizard, cried exactly like Stasee when she knew that Sister Sarah couldn't see her after service anymore, when Priest McCarthy was done using her. Jonny sobbed most like the moment he heard that Stasee had jumped off of the Aurora Bridge. Jonny's tears eventually turned into snores, as he was exhausted from the weekend. He hadn't slept much since Thursday, the day that David and Amanda had flown into LAX. Luckily, David and Amanda knew Jonny well enough to make sure that they set the alarm on his iPhone to 3:00 in the afternoon. Jonny's flight to Seattle left at 6:50 that evening.

Jonny sat in the airport despondent awaiting his flight anxiously he awaited boarding so he could continue sleeping on the plane. The night and the morning and Saint Mary's Church and even how he got to the airport were a blur. He forgot that he made the taxi driver pull over on the Fourth Street Bridge so he could puke into the Los Angeles River. He forgot not tipping the congenial, tolerant, and amiable taxi driver. He forgot that he alienated just about everyone on his block. He just remembered Stasee.

David and Amanda picked him up from Sea-Tac Airport and they drove straight to the Aurora Bridge. They

already knew what was on each other's minds so instinctively none of them spoke. Until Jonny broke the silence,
"If there is a heaven... Stasee is there."
They sat there quietly for the rest of the night.

About the Author

Jonathan Sheppard is a Seattle born writer, based in Los Angeles. He primarily writes cynical, brooding, dark, and angstsy introspective poetry that occasionally delves into a macro understanding of self and society but he also writes similarly themed essays and short stories. Jonathan has a Bachelor's degree in English from UCLA. He has written three books of poetry, and one book of short stories, *Bad Stories*.

INSTAGRAM: @iamjonathansheppard
EMAIL: chiefjonny@badthoughtspublishing.com
WEBSITE: http://www.jonathansheppard.org

www.ingramcontent.com/pod-product-compliance
Lightning Source LLC
Chambersburg PA
CBHW030114170426
43198CB00009B/615